12|15.

MRS
BEETON'S
GUIDE
TO
BAKING

MRS BEETON'S GUIDE TO BAKING

ISABELLA BEETON
EDITED BY G. COLEBY

AMBERLEY

First published 1861
This edition first published 2015

Amberley Publishing
The Hill, Stroud
Gloucestershire, GL5 4EP

www.amberley-books.com

British Library Cataloguing in Publication Data.
A catalogue record for this book is available from the British Library.

ISBN 978 1 4456 5106 4 (hardback)
ISBN 978 1 4456 5107 1 (ebook)

Typeset in 9.5pt on 11.5pt Sabon.
Typesetting and Origination by Fakenham Prepress Solutions.
Printed in the UK.

Contents

Editor's Note

This book contains a compilation of Mrs Beeton's advice about, and recipes for, baking, taken from the first edition of her *Book of Household Management*, published in 1861. It begins with the best of her hints and tips, moves on to recipes that are suitable for cooking all year round and ends with a collection of recipes for each season, each ordered by their main ingredient. Where recipes are designated suitable for more than one season, they are allocated to the season that occurs first. While much of the advice, and indeed the recipes, are still valid and useful in today's kitchen, there are some elements that are less relevant in modern times and which wouldn't necessarily be sensible to follow. For example, we would be unlikely these days to sew up a stuffed fish in order to bake it, or to use cartridge paper to bake with (greaseproof being a much better modern alternative). However, some the basics remain the same, and in both advice and recipes we are given a fascinating insight into Victorian baking, in which we find the roots of the modern equivalent. Mrs Beeton's original language and spellings have been retained throughout and her recipes presented as she originally put them for the first edition of the *Book of Household Management*, as far as possible, so a little modern interpretation is usually required in order to use the advice and recipes.

The Advice

Equipment

Among the most essential requirements of the kitchen are scales or weighing machines for family use. These are found to have existed among the ancients, and must, at a very early age, have been both publicly and privately employed for the regulation of quantities. The modern English weights were adjusted by the twenty-seventh chapter of Magna Carta, or the great charter forced, by the barons, from King John at Runnymede, in Surrey. Therein, it is declared that the weights all over England shall be the same, although for different commodities there were two different kinds, Troy and Avoirdupois. The origin of both is taken from a grain of wheat gathered in the middle of an ear. The standard of measures was originally kept at Winchester, and by a law of King Edgar was ordained to be observed throughout the kingdom.

Accompanying the scales, or weighing machines, there should be spice boxes and sugar and biscuit canisters of either white or japanned tin. The covers of these should fit tightly, in order to exclude the air, and if necessary, be lettered in front to distinguish them. The white metal of which they are usually composed loses its colour when exposed to the air, but undergoes no further change. It enters largely into the composition of culinary utensils, many of them being entirely composed of tinned sheet-iron; the inside of copper and iron vessels also, being usually what is called tinned. This art consists of covering any metal with a thin coating of tin, and it requires the metal to be covered, to be perfectly clean and free from rust and also that the tin, itself, be purely metallic and entirely cleared from all ashes or refuse. Copper boilers, saucepans, and other kitchen utensils are tinned after they are manufactured, by being first made hot and the tin rubbed on with resin. In this process, nothing ought to be used but pure grain-tin. Lead, however, is sometimes mixed with that metal, not only to make it lie more easily, but to adulterate it – a pernicious practice, which in every article connected with the cooking and preparation of food, cannot be too severely reprobated.

As not only health but life may be said to depend on the cleanliness of culinary utensils, great attention must be paid to their condition generally, but more especially to that of the saucepans, stewpans, and boilers. Inside they should be kept perfectly clean, and where an open fire is used, keep the outside as clean as possible. With a Leamington range, saucepans, stewpans, etc., can be kept entirely free from smoke and soot on the outside, which is an immense saving of labour to the cook or scullery maid. Care should be taken that the lids fit tightly and close, so that soups or gravies may not be suffered to waste by evaporation. They should be made to keep the steam in and the smoke out, and should always be bright on the upper rim where they do not immediately come in contact with the fire. Soup-pots and kettles should be washed immediately after being used, and dried before the fire, and they should be kept in a dry place in order that they may escape the deteriorating influence of rust, and, thereby, be destroyed. Copper utensils should never be used in the kitchen unless tinned, and the utmost care should be taken not to let the tin be rubbed off. If by chance this should occur, have it replaced before the vessel is again brought into use. Neither soup nor gravy should, at any time, be suffered to remain in them longer than is absolutely necessary, as any fat or acid which is in them may affect the metal, so as to impregnate with poison what is intended to be eaten. Stone and earthenware vessels should be provided for soups and gravies not intended for immediate use and also for plenty of common dishes for the larder, that the table-set may not be used for such purposes. It is the nature of vegetables soon to turn sour, when they are apt to corrode glazed red ware, and even metals, and frequently, thereby, to become impregnated with poisonous particles. The vinegar in pickles, by its acidity, does the same. Consideration, therefore, should be given to these facts, and great care also taken that all sieves, jelly-bags and tapes for collared articles be well scalded and kept dry, or they will impart an unpleasant flavour when next used. To all these directions, the cook should pay great attention, nor should they, by any means, be neglected by the mistress of the household who ought to remember that cleanliness in the kitchen gives health and happiness to the home, while economy will immeasurably assist in preserving them.

Without fuel, a Kitchen might be pronounced to be of little use; therefore, to discover and invent materials for supplying us with the means of domestic heat and comfort, has exercised the ingenuity of man. Those now known have been divided into five classes: the first, comprehending the fluid inflammable bodies; the second, peat or turf; the third, charcoal of wood; the fourth, pit-coal charred and the fifth, wood or pit-coal in a crude state, with the capacity of yielding a copious and bright flame. The first may be said seldom to be employed for the purposes of cookery, but peat, especially amongst rural populations, has, in all ages, been regarded as an excellent fuel. It is one of the most important productions of an alluvial soil and belongs to the vegetable rather than the mineral kingdom. It may be described as composed of wet, spongy black earth held together by decayed vegetables. Formerly, it covered extensive tracts in England but has greatly disappeared before the genius of agricultural improvement. Charcoal is a kind of artificial coal used principally where a strong and clear fire is desired. It is a black, brittle, insoluble, inodorous, tasteless substance, and, when newly made, possesses the remarkable property of absorbing certain quantities of the different gases. Its dust, when used as a polishing powder, gives great brilliancy to metals. It consists of wood half-burned, and is manufactured by cutting pieces of timber into nearly the same size, then disposing them in heaps and covering them with earth, so as to prevent communication with the air, except when necessary to make them burn. When they have been sufficiently charred, the fire is extinguished by stopping the vents through which the air is admitted. Of coal, there are such various species as pit, culm, slate, cannel, Kilkenny, sulphurous, bovey, jet, etc. These have all their specific differences and are employed for various purposes, but are all, more or less, used as fuel.

The use of coal for burning purposes was not known to the Romans. In Britain, it was discovered about fifty years before the birth of Christ, in Lancashire, not far from where Manchester now stands, but for ages after its discovery, so long as forests abounded, wood continued to be the fuel used for firing. The first public notice of coal is in the reign of Henry III, who, in 1272, granted a charter to the town of Newcastle, permitting the inhabitants to dig for coal. It took some centuries more, however, to bring it into common use, as this did not take place till about the first quarter of the seventeenth century, in the time of Charles I. A few years after the Restoration, we find that about 200,000 chaldrons were consumed in London. Although several countries possess mines of coal, the quality of their mineral is, in general, greatly inferior to that of Great Britain, where it is found mostly in undulating districts abounding with valleys and interspersed with plains of considerable extent. It lies usually between the strata of other substances, and rarely in an horizontal position, but with a dip or inclination to one side.

General Observations on Bread, Biscuits and Cakes

Bread and Bread Making

Among the numerous vegetable products yielding articles of food for man, the cereals (a corn-producing plant; from Ceres, the goddess of agriculture) hold the first place. By means of skilful cultivation, mankind have transformed the original forms of these growths, poor and ill-flavoured as they perhaps were, into various fruitful and agreeable species, which yield an abundant and pleasant supply. Classified according to their respective richness in alimentary elements, the cereals stand thus: Wheat, and its varieties, Rye, Barley, Oats, Rice, and Indian Corn. Everybody knows it is wheat flour that yields the best bread. Rye bread is viscous, hard, less easily soluble by the gastric juice and not so rich in nutritive power. Flour produced from Barley, Indian Corn, or Rice, is not so readily made into bread; and the article, when made, is heavy and indigestible.

On examining a grain of corn from any of the numerous cereals used in the preparation of flour, such as wheat, maize, barley, etc., it will be found to consist of two parts: the husk, or exterior covering, which is generally of a dark colour, and the inner, or albuminous part, which is more or less white. In grinding, these two portions are separated and the husk being blown away in the process of winnowing, the flour remains in the form of a light brown powder, consisting principally of starch and gluten. In order to render it white, it undergoes a process called 'bolting'. It is passed through a series of fine sieves, which separate the coarser parts, leaving behind fine white flour, the 'fine firsts' of the corn dealer. The process of bolting, as just described, tends to deprive flour of its gluten, the coarser and darker portion containing much of that substance, while the lighter part is peculiarly rich in starch. Bran contains a large proportion of gluten, hence it will be seen why brown bread is so much more

WHEAT.

nutritious than white; in fact we may lay it down as a general rule that the whiter the bread the less nourishment it contains. Majendie proved this by feeding a dog for forty days with white wheaten bread, at the end of which time he died; while another dog fed on brown bread made with flour mixed with bran lived without any disturbance of his health. The bolting process, then, is rather injurious than beneficial and is one of the numerous instances where fashion has chosen a wrong standard to go by. In ancient times, down to the Emperors, no bolted flour was known. In many parts of Germany, the entire meal is used, and in no part of the world are the digestive organs of the people in a better condition. In years of famine, when corn is scarce, the use of bolted flour is most culpable, for from 18 to 20 per cent is lost in bran. Brown bread has, of late years, become very popular, and many physicians have recommended it to invalids with weak digestions with great success. This rage for white bread has introduced adulterations of a very serious character, affecting the health of the whole community. Potatoes are added for this purpose; but this is a comparatively harmless cheat, only reducing the nutritive property of the bread; but bone dust and alum are also put in, which are far from harmless.

Bread making is a very ancient art indeed. The Assyrians, Egyptians and Greeks used to make bread, in which oil, with aniseed and other spices, was an element, but this was unleavened. Every family used to prepare the bread for its own consumption, the *trade* of baking not having yet taken shape. It is said that somewhere about the beginning of the thirtieth Olympiad, the slave of an archon, at Athens, made leavened bread by accident. He had left some wheaten dough in an earthen pan and forgotten it; some days afterwards, he lighted upon it again and found it turning sour. His first thought was to throw it away, but, his master coming up, he mixed this now acescent dough with some fresh dough, which he was working at. The bread thus produced, by the introduction of dough in which alcoholic fermentation had begun, was found delicious by the archon and his friends; and the slave, being summoned and catechised, told the secret. It spread all over Athens, and everybody wanting leavened bread at once, certain persons set up as bread makers or bakers. In a short time, bread baking became quite an art and 'Athenian bread' was quoted all over Greece as the best bread, just as the honey of Hymettus was celebrated as the best honey.

In our own times, and among civilised peoples, bread has become an article of food of the first necessity; and properly so, for it constitutes of itself a complete life-sustainer, the gluten, starch and sugar that it contains representing azotised and hydrocarbonated nutrients, and combining the sustaining powers of the animal and vegetable kingdoms in one product.

Wheaten Bread

The finest, wholesomest, and most savoury bread is made from wheaten flour. There are, of wheat, three leading qualities: the soft, the medium and the hard wheat, the last of which yields a kind of bread that is not so white as that made from soft wheat, but is richer in gluten, and consequently more nutritive.

Rye Bread

This comes next to wheaten bread; it is not so rich in gluten but is said to keep fresh longer and to have some laxative qualities.

Barley Bread, Indian Corn Bread, etc.

Bread made from barley, maize, oats, rice, potatoes, etc., 'rises' badly, because the grains in question contain but little gluten, which makes the bread heavy, close in texture and difficult of digestion; in fact, cornflour has to be added before panification can take place. In countries where wheat is scarce

MAIZE PLANT.

and maize abundant, the people make the latter a chief article of sustenance when prepared in different forms.

Bread Making

Panification, or bread-making, consists of the following processes, in the case of Wheaten Flour. 50 or 60 per cent of water is added to the flour, with the addition of some leavening matter, and, preferably, of yeast from malt and hops. All kinds of leavening matter have, however, been, and are still used in different parts of the world. In the East Indies, 'toddy', which is a liquor that flows from the wounded cocoa-nut tree, and in the West Indies, 'dunder', or the refuse of the distillation of rum. The dough then undergoes the well-known process called *kneading*. The yeast produces fermentation, a process which may be thus described: the dough reacting upon the leavening matter introduced, the starch of the flour is transformed into saccharine matter, the saccharine matter being afterwards changed into alcohol and carbonic acid. The dough must be well 'bound' and yet not allow the escape of the little bubbles of carbonic acid which accompany the fermentation, and which, in their passage, cause the numerous little holes that are seen in light bread.

The yeast must be good and fresh if the bread is to be digestible and nice. Stale yeast produces, instead of vinous fermentation, an acetous fermentation, which flavours the bread and makes it disagreeable. A poor thin yeast produces an imperfect fermentation, the result being a heavy, unwholesome loaf.

When the dough is well kneaded, it is left to stand for some time, and then, as soon as it begins to swell, it is divided into loaves, after which it is again left to stand, when it once more swells up, and manifests, for the last time, the symptoms of fermentation. It is then put into the oven, where the water contained in the dough is partly evaporated and the loaves swell up again, while a yellow crust begins to form upon the surface. When the bread is sufficiently baked, the bottom crust is hard and resonant if struck with the finger, while the crumb is elastic and rises again after being pressed down with the finger. The bread is, in all probability, baked sufficiently if, on opening the door of the oven, you are met by a cloud of steam which quickly passes away.

One word as to the unwholesomeness of new bread and hot rolls. When bread is taken out of the oven, it is full of moisture; the starch is held together in masses, and the bread, instead of being crusted so as to expose each grain of starch to the saliva, actually prevents their digestion by being formed by the teeth into leathery poreless masses, which lie on the stomach like so many bullets. Bread should always be at least a day old before it is eaten and, if properly made and kept in a *cool dry* place, ought to be perfectly soft and palatable at the end of three or four days. Hot rolls, swimming in melted butter, and new bread ought to be carefully shunned by everybody who has the slightest respect for that much-injured individual – the stomach.

Aerated Bread

It is not unknown to some of our readers that Dr Dauglish, of Malvern, has recently patented a process for making bread 'light' without of leaven. The ordinary process of bread making by fermentation is tedious, and much labour of human hands is requisite in the kneading, in order that the dough may be thoroughly interpenetrated with the leaven. The new process impregnates the bread by the application of machinery, with carbonic acid gas or fixed air. Different opinions are expressed about the bread, but it is curious to note that as corn is now reaped by machinery and dough is baked by machinery, the whole process of bread making is probably in course of undergoing changes that will emancipate both the housewife and the professional baker from a large amount of labour.

In the production of Aerated Bread, wheaten flour, water, salt, and carbonic acid gas (generated by proper machinery) are the only materials employed. We need not inform our readers that carbonic acid gas is the source of the effervescence, whether in common water coming from a depth, or in lemonade, or any aerated drink. Its action, in the new bread, takes the place of fermentation in the old.

AERATED BREAD.

In the patent process, the dough is mixed in a great iron ball, inside which is a system of paddles, perpetually turning and doing the kneading part of the business. Into this globe, the flour is dropped till it is full and then the common atmospheric air is pumped out and the pure gas turned on. The gas is followed by the water, which has been aerated for the purpose, and then begins the churning or kneading part of the business.

Of course, it is not long before we have the dough, and very 'light' and nice it looks. This is caught in tins, and passed on to the floor of the oven, which is an endless floor, moving slowly through the fire. Done to a turn, the loaves emerge at the other end of the apartment and the Aerated Bread is made.

It may be added that it is a good plan to change one's baker from time to time and so secure a change in the quality of the bread that is eaten.

Mixed Breads

Rye bread is hard of digestion, and requires longer and slower baking than wheaten bread. It is better when made with leaven of wheaten flour rather than yeast and turns out lighter. It should not be eaten till two days old. It will keep a long time.

A good bread may be made by mixing rye flour, wheat flour and rice paste in equal proportions; also by mixing rye, wheat and barley. In Norway, it is said that they only bake their barley bread once a year, such is its 'keeping' quality.

Indian Corn flour mixed with wheat flour (half with half) makes a nice bread, but it is not considered very digestible, though it keeps well.

Rice cannot be made into bread, nor can potatoes, but one-third potato flour to three-fourths wheaten flour makes a tolerably good loaf.

A very good bread, better than the ordinary sort, and of a delicious flavour, is said to be produced by adopting the following recipe. Take ten parts of wheat flour, five parts of potato flour, one part of rice paste; knead together, add the yeast, and bake as usual. This is, of course, cheaper than wheaten bread.

Flour, when freshly ground, is too glutinous to make good bread and should therefore not be used immediately, but should be kept dry for a few weeks, and stirred occasionally, until it becomes dry and crumbles easily between the fingers.

Flour should be perfectly dry before being used for bread or cakes; if at all damp, the preparation is sure to be heavy. Before mixing it with the other ingredients, it is a good plan to place it for an hour or two before the fire, until it feels warm and dry.

Yeast from home-brewed beer is generally preferred to any other; it is very bitter and, on that account, should be well washed and put away until the thick mass settles. If it still continues bitter, the process should be repeated, and, before being used, all the water floating at the top must be poured off. German yeast is now very much used, and should be moistened, and thoroughly mixed with the milk or water with which the bread is to be made.

The following observations are extracted from *The English Bread Book* by Eliza Acton, a valuable work on bread making, and will be found very useful to our readers:

The first thing required for making wholesome bread is the utmost cleanliness; the next is the soundness and sweetness of all the ingredients used for it and, in addition to these, there must be attention and care throughout the whole process.

An almost certain way of spoiling dough is to leave it half made and to allow it to become cold before it is finished. The other most common causes of failure are using yeast that is no longer sweet, or that has been frozen, or that has had hot liquid poured over it.

Too small a proportion of yeast, or insufficient time allowed for the dough to rise, will cause the bread to be heavy.

Heavy bread will also most likely be the result of making the dough very hard and letting it become quite cold, particularly in winter.

If either the sponge or the dough be permitted to overwork itself, that is to say, if the mixing and kneading be neglected when it has reached the proper point for either, sour bread will probably be the consequence in warm weather, and bad bread in any. The goodness will also be endangered by placing it so near a fire as to make any part of it hot, instead of maintaining the gentle and equal degree of heat required for its due fermentation.

To keep bread sweet and fresh, as soon as it is cold, it should be put into a clean earthen pan, with a cover to it; this pan should be placed at a little distance from the ground to allow a current of air to pass underneath. Some persons prefer keeping bread on clean wooden shelves, without being covered, that the crust may not soften. Stale bread may be freshened by warming it through in a gentle oven. Stale pastry, cakes, etc., may also be improved by this method.

The utensils required for making bread, on a moderate scale, are a kneading trough or pan, sufficiently large that the dough may be kneaded freely without throwing the flour over the edges and also to allow for its rising; a hair sieve for straining yeast and one or two strong spoons.

Yeast must always be good of its kind, and in a fitting state to produce ready and proper fermentation. Yeast of strong beer or ale produces more effect than that of milder kinds, and the fresher the yeast, the smaller the quantity that will be required to raise the dough.

As a general rule, the oven for baking bread should be rather quick, and the heat so regulated as to penetrate the dough without hardening the outside. The oven door should not be opened after the bread is put in until the dough is set, or has become firm, as the cool air admitted will have an unfavourable effect on it.

Brick ovens are generally considered the best adapted for baking bread: these should be heated with wood faggots, and then swept and mopped out, to cleanse them for the reception of the bread. Iron ovens are more difficult to manage, being apt to burn the surface of the bread before the middle is baked. To remedy this, a few clean bricks should be set at the bottom of the oven, close together, to receive the tins of bread. In many modern stoves, the ovens are so much improved that they bake admirably, and they can always be brought to the required temperature, when it is higher than is needed, by leaving the door open for a time.

Milk or Butter

Milk which is not perfectly sweet will not only injure the flavour of the bread but, in sultry weather, will often cause it to be quite uneatable; yet either of them (milk or butter), if *fresh and good*, will materially improve its quality.

Bread Making in Spain

The bread in the south of Spain is delicious: it is white as snow, close as cake, and yet very light; the flavour is most admirable, for the wheat is good and pure, and the bread well kneaded. The way they make this bread is as follows: from large round panniers filled with wheat they take out a handful at a time, sorting it most carefully and expeditiously, and throwing every defective grain into another basket. This done, the wheat is ground between two circular stones, as it was ground in Egypt 2,000 years ago, the requisite rotary motion being given by a blindfolded mule, which paces round and round with untiring patience, a bell being attached to his neck, which, as long as he is in movement, tinkles on, and when it stops, he is urged to his duty by the shout of 'Arre, mula', from someone within hearing. When ground, the wheat is sifted through three sieves, the last of these being so fine that only the pure flour can pass through it: this is of a pale apricot colour. The bread is made in the evening. It is mixed only with sufficient water, with a little salt in it, to make it into dough: a very small quantity of leaven, or fermenting mixture, is added. The Scripture says, 'A little leaven leaveneth the whole lump;' but in England, to avoid the trouble of kneading, many put as much leaven or yeast in one batch of household bread, as in Spain would last them a week for the six or eight donkey loads of bread they send every night from their oven. The dough made, it is put into sacks and carried on the donkeys' backs to the oven in the centre of the village, so as to bake it immediately it is kneaded. On arriving there, the dough is divided into portions weighing 3 lbs each. Two long narrow wooden tables on trestles are then placed down thee room, and now a curious sight may be seen. About twenty men (bakers) come in and range themselves on one side of the tables. A lump of dough is handed to the nearest, which he commences kneading and knocking about with all his might for about 3 or 4 minutes, and then passes it on to his neighbour, who does the same; and so on successively until all have kneaded it, when it becomes as soft as new putty and ready for the oven. Of course, as soon as the first baker has handed the first lump to his neighbour, another is given to him, and so on till the whole quantity of dough is successively kneaded by them all. The bakers' wives and daughters shape the loaves for the oven and some of them are very small and they are baked immediately. The ovens are very large and not heated by fires *under* them; but a quantity of twigs of the herbs of sweet marjoram and thyme, which cover the hills in great profusion, are put in the oven and ignited. They heat the oven to the extent required, and as the bread gets baked, the oven gets gradually colder, so the bread is never burned. They knead the bread in Spain with such force that the palm of the hand and the second joints of the fingers of the bakers are covered with corns, and it so affects the chest that they cannot work more than 2 hours at a time.

A Few Hints Respecting the Making and Baking of Cakes

Eggs should always be broken into a cup, the whites and yolks separated, and they should always be strained. Breaking the eggs thus, the bad ones may be easily rejected without spoiling the others and so cause no waste. As eggs are used instead of yeast, they should be very thoroughly whisked; they are generally sufficiently beaten when thick enough to carry the drop that falls from the whisk.

Loaf sugar should be well pounded and then sifted through a fine sieve.

Currants should be nicely washed, picked, dried in a cloth, and then carefully examined that no pieces of grit or stone may be left among them. They should then be laid on a dish before the fire to become thoroughly dry, as, if added damp to the other ingredients, cakes will be liable to be heavy.

Good butter should always be used in the manufacture of cakes and, if beaten to a cream, it saves much time and labour to warm, but not melt, it before beating.

Less butter and eggs are required for cakes when yeast is mixed with the other ingredients.

The heat of the oven is of great importance, especially for large cakes. If the heat be not tolerably fierce, the batter will not rise. If the oven is too quick, and there is any danger of the cake burning or catching, put a sheet of clean paper over the top. Newspaper, or paper that has been printed on, should never be used for this purpose.

To know when a cake sufficiently baked, plunge a clean knife into the middle of it; draw it quickly out and if it looks in the least sticky, put the cake back and close the oven door until the cake is done.

Cakes should be kept in closed tin canisters or jars and in a dry place. Those made with yeast do not keep so long as those made without it.

Biscuits

Since the establishment of the large modern biscuit manufactories, biscuits have been produced both cheap and wholesome, in, comparatively speaking, endless variety. Their actual component parts are, perhaps, known only to the various makers, but there are several kinds of biscuits that have long been in use, which may here be advantageously described.

Biscuits belong to the class of unfermented bread and are, perhaps, the most wholesome of that class. In cases where fermented bread does not agree with the human stomach, they may be recommended: in many instances they are considered lighter and less liable to create acidity and flatulence. The name is derived from the French *bis cuit*, 'twice baked', because, originally, that was the mode of entirely depriving them of all moisture to insure their keeping; but, although that process is no longer employed, the name is retained. The use of this kind of bread on land is pretty general, and some varieties are luxuries; but at sea, biscuits are articles of the first necessity.

Sea, or ship biscuits, are made of wheat flour from which only the coarsest bran has been separated. The dough is made up as stiff as it can be worked and is then formed into shapes and baked in an oven; after which, the biscuits are exposed in lofts over the oven until perfectly dry to prevent them from becoming mouldy when stored.

Captains' biscuits are made in a similar manner, only of fine flour.

General Observations on Puddings and Pastry

Puddings and pastry, familiar as they may be and unimportant as they may be held in the estimation of some, are yet intimately connected with the development of agricultural resources in reference to the cereal grasses. When they began to be made is uncertain, but we may safely presume that a simple form of pudding was amongst the first dishes made after discovering a mode of grinding wheat to flour. As to who was the real discoverer of the use of corn, we have no authentic knowledge. The traditions of different countries ascribe it to various personages, whose names it is here unnecessary to introduce. In Egypt, however, corn must have grown abundantly, for Abraham, and after him Jacob, had recourse to that country for supplies during times of famine.

The habits of a people, to a great extent, are formed by the climate in which they live and by the native or cultivated productions in which their country abounds. Thus we find that the agricultural produce of the ancient Egyptians is pretty much the same as that of the present day, and the habits of the people are not materially altered. In Greece, the products cultivated in antiquity were the same kinds of grains and legumes as are cultivated at present, with the vine, the fig, the olive, the apple and other fruits; so with the Romans and so with other nations. As to the different modes of artificially preparing these to please the taste, it is only necessary to say that they arise from the universal desire of novelty, characteristic of man in the development of his social conditions. Thus has arisen the whole science of cookery and thus arose the art of making puddings. The porridge of the Scotch is nothing more than a species of hasty pudding, composed of oatmeal, salt, and water, and the 'red pottage' for which Esau sold his birthright must have been something similar. The barley gruel of the Lacedaemonians, of the Athenian gladiators and common people, was the same, with the exception of the slight seasoning it had beyond the simplicity of Scottish fare. Here is the ancient recipe for the Athenian national dish: 'Dry near the fire, in the oven, twenty pounds of barley flour; then parch it; add three pounds of linseed meal, half a pound of coriander seed, two ounces of salt, and the quantity of water necessary'. To this sometimes a little millet was added in order to give the paste greater cohesion and delicacy.

Oatmeal amongst the Greeks and Roman was highly esteemed, as was also rice, which they considered as beneficial to the chest. They also held in high repute the Iron or Indian wheat of the moderns. The flour of this cereal was made into a kind of hasty pudding and, parched or roasted, was eaten with a little salt. The Spelt, or Red wheat, was likewise esteemed, and its flour formed the basis of the Carthaginian pudding, for which we here give the scientific recipe: 'Put a pound of red wheat flour into water, and when it has steeped for some time, transfer it to a wooden bowl. Add three pounds of cream cheese, half a pound of honey and one egg. Beat the whole together, and cook it on a slow fire in a stewpan.' Should this be considered unpalatable, another form has been recommended. 'Sift the flour and, with some water, put it into a wooden vessel and, for ten days, renew the water twice each day. At the end of that period, press out the water and place the paste in another vessel. It is now to be reduced to the consistence of thick lees and passed through a piece of new linen. Repeat this last operation, then dry the mass in the sun and boil it in the milk. Season according to taste.' These are specimens of the puddings of antiquity, and this last recipe was held in especial favour by the Romans.

However great may have been the qualifications of the ancients, however, in the art of pudding making, we apprehend that such preparations as gave gratification to their palates, would have generally found little favour among the insulated inhabitants of Great Britain. Here, from the simple suet dumpling up to the most complicated Christmas production, the grand feature of substantiality is primarily attended to. Variety in the ingredients, we think, is held only of secondary consideration with the great body of the people, provided that the whole is agreeable and of sufficient abundance.

Although from puddings to pastry is but a step, it requires a higher degree of art to make the one than to make the other. Indeed, pastry is one of the most important branches of the culinary science. It unceasingly occupies itself with ministering pleasure to the sight as well as to the taste, with erecting graceful monuments, miniature fortresses and all kinds of architectural imitations, composed of the sweetest and most agreeable products of all climates and countries. At a very early period, the Orientals were acquainted with the art of manipulating in pastry, but they by no means attained to the taste, variety and splendour of design, by which it is characterised amongst the moderns. At first it generally consisted of certain mixtures of flour, oil, and honey, to which it was confined for centuries, even among the southern nations of the European continent. At the commencement of the middle ages, a change began to take place in the art of mixing it. Eggs, butter and salt came into repute in the making of paste, which was forthwith used as an inclosure for meat, seasoned with spices. This advance attained, the next step was to inclose cream, fruit and marmalades, and the next, to build pyramids and castles; when the summit of the art of the pastry cook may be supposed to have been achieved.

Directions in Connection with the Making of Puddings and Pastry

Flour should be of the best quality, and perfectly dry, and sifted before being used; if in the least damp, the paste made from it will certainly be heavy.

Butter, unless fresh is used, should be washed from the salt and well squeezed and wrung in a cloth, to get out all the water and buttermilk, which, if left in, assists to make the paste heavy.

Lard should be perfectly sweet, which may be ascertained by cutting the bladder through, and, if the knife smells sweet, the lard is good.

Suet should be finely chopped, perfectly free from skin and quite sweet; during the process of chopping, it should be lightly dredged with flour, which prevents the pieces from sticking together. Beef suet is considered the best, but veal suet, or the outside fat of a loin or neck of mutton, makes good crusts; as also the skimmings in which a joint of mutton has been boiled but *without vegetables*.

Clarified beef dripping answers very well for kitchen pies, puddings, cakes or for family use. A very good short crust may be made by mixing with it a small quantity of moist sugar, but care must be taken to use the dripping sparingly or a very disagreeable flavour will be imparted to the taste.

Strict cleanliness must be observed in pastry making; all the utensils used should be perfectly free from dust and dirt, and the things required for pastry kept entirely for that purpose.

In mixing paste, add the water very gradually, work the whole together with the knife blade and knead it until perfectly smooth. Those who are inexperienced in pastry making should work the butter in by breaking it in small pieces and covering the paste rolled out. It should then be dredged with flour and the ends folded over and rolled very thin again: this process must be repeated until all the butter is used.

The art of making paste requires much practice, dexterity and skill: it should be touched as lightly as possible, made with cool hands and in a cool place (a marble slab is better than a board for the purpose), and the coolest part of the house should be selected for the process during warm weather.

To insure rich paste being light, great expedition must be used in the making and baking; for if it stand long before it is put in the oven, it becomes flat and heavy.

Puff paste requires a brisk oven, but not too hot, or it would blacken the crust; on the other hand, if the oven be too slack, the paste will be soddened, and will not rise, nor will it have any colour.

Tart tins, cake moulds, dishes for baked puddings, pattypans, etc., should all be buttered before the article intended to be baked is put in them: things to be baked on sheets should be placed on buttered paper. Raised pie paste should have a soaking heat, and paste glazed must have rather a slack oven, that the icing be not scorched. It is better to ice tarts, etc., when they are three parts baked.

To ascertain when the oven is heated to the proper degree for puff paste, put a small piece of the paste in previous to baking the whole and then the heat can thus be judged of.

The freshness of all pudding ingredients is of much importance, as one bad article will taint the whole mixture.

When the freshness of eggs is doubtful, break each one separately in a cup, before mixing them altogether. Should there be a bad one among them, it can be thrown away; whereas, if mixed with the good ones, the entire quantity would be spoiled. The yolks and whites beaten separately make the articles they are put into much lighter.

Raisins and dried fruits for puddings should be carefully picked and, in many cases, stoned. Currants should be well washed, pressed in a cloth and placed on a dish before the fire to get thoroughly dry; they should then be picked carefully over and every piece of grit or stone removed from amongst them. To plump them, some cooks pour boiling water over them and then dry them before the fire.

Batter pudding should be smoothly mixed and free from lumps. To insure this, first mix the flour with a very small proportion of milk and add the remainder by degrees. Should the pudding be very lumpy, it may be strained through a hair sieve.

All boiled puddings should be put on in boiling water, which must not be allowed to stop simmering, and the pudding must always be covered with the water; if requisite, the saucepan should be kept filled up.

To prevent a pudding boiled in a cloth from sticking to the bottom of the saucepan, place a small plate or saucer underneath it and set the pan on a trivet over the fire. If a mould is used, this precaution is not necessary; but care must be taken to keep the pudding well covered with water.

For dishing a boiled pudding as soon as it comes out of the pot, dip it into a basin of cold water, and the cloth will then not adhere to it. Great expedition is necessary in sending puddings to table, as, by standing, they quickly become heavy, batter puddings particularly.

For baked or boiled puddings, the moulds, cups or basins should be always buttered before the mixture is put in them and they should be put into the saucepan directly they are filled.

Scrupulous attention should be paid to the cleanliness of pudding cloths, as, from neglect in this particular, the outsides of boiled puddings frequently taste very disagreeably. As soon as possible after it is taken off the pudding, it should be soaked in water and then well washed, without soap, unless it be very greasy. It should be dried out of doors, then folded up and kept in a dry place. When wanted for use, dip it in boiling water, and dredge it slightly with flour.

The dry ingredients for puddings are better for being mixed some time before they are wanted; the liquid portion should only be added just before the pudding is put into the saucepan.

A pinch of salt is an improvement to the generality of puddings; but this ingredient should be added very sparingly, as the flavour should not be detected.

When baked puddings are sufficiently solid, turn them out of the dish they were baked in, bottom uppermost, and strew over them fine sifted sugar.

When pastry or baked puddings are not done through, and yet the outer side is sufficiently brown, cover them over with a piece of white paper until thoroughly cooked: this prevents them from getting burnt.

Soufflés, Omelets, and Sweet Dishes, in which eggs form the principal ingredient, demand, for their successful manufacture, an experienced cook. They are the prettiest but most difficult of all entremets. The most essential thing to insure success is to secure the best ingredients from an honest tradesman. The entremets coming within the above classification are healthy, nourishing and pleasant to the taste and may be eaten with safety by persons of the most delicate stomachs.

Dessert Dishes

With moderns, the dessert is not so profuse nor does it hold the same relationship to the dinner that it held with the ancients, the Romans more especially. On ivory tables, they would spread hundreds of different kinds of raw, cooked and preserved fruits, tarts and cakes, as substitutes for the more substantial comestibles with which the guests were satiated. However, as late as the reigns of our two last Georges, fabulous sums were often expended upon fanciful desserts. The dessert certainly repays, in its general effect, the expenditure upon it of much pains, and it may be said that if there be any poetry at all in meals, or the process of feeding, there is poetry in the dessert, the materials for which should be selected with taste and, of course, must depend, in a great measure, upon the season. Pines, melons, grapes, peaches, nectarines, plums, strawberries, apples, pears, oranges, almonds, raisins, figs, walnuts, filberts, medlars, cherries, etc., all kinds of dried fruits and choice and delicately flavoured cakes and biscuits make up the dessert, together with the most costly and recherché wines. The shape of the dishes varies at different periods, the prevailing fashion at present being oval and circular dishes on stems. The patterns and colours are also subject to changes of fashion; some persons selecting china, chaste in pattern and colour; others, elegantly shaped glass dishes on stems, with gilt edges. The beauty of the dessert services at the tables of the wealthy tends to enhance the splendour of the plate. The general mode of putting a dessert on table, now the elegant tazzas are fashionable, is to place them down the middle of the table, a tall and short dish alternately; the fresh fruits being arranged on the tall dishes, and dried fruits, bon-bons, etc., on small round or oval glass plates. The garnishing needs especial attention, as the contrast of the brilliant-coloured fruits with nicely arranged foliage is very charming. The garnish *par excellence* for dessert is the ice plant; its crystallised dew drops producing a marvellous effect in the height of summer, giving a most inviting sense of coolness to the fruit it encircles. The double-edged mallow, strawberry and vine leaves have a pleasing effect; and for winter desserts, the bay, cuba and laurel are sometimes used. In town, the expense and difficulty of obtaining natural foliage is great, but paper and composite leaves are to be purchased at an almost nominal price. Mixed fruits of the larger sort are now frequently served on one dish. This mode admits of the display of much taste in the arrangement of the fruit: for instance, a pine in the centre of the dish, surrounded with large plums of various sorts and colours, mixed with pears and rosy-cheeked apples, all arranged with a due regard to colour, have a very good effect. Again, apples and pears look well mingled with plums and grapes, hanging from the border of the dish in a *négligé* sort of manner, with a large bunch of the same fruit lying on the top of the apples. A dessert would not now be considered complete without candied and preserved fruits and confections. The candied fruits may be purchased at a lesser cost than they can be manufactured at home. They are preserved abroad in most ornamental and elegant forms. And since, from the facilities of travel, we have become so familiar with the tables of the French, chocolate in different forms is indispensable to our desserts.

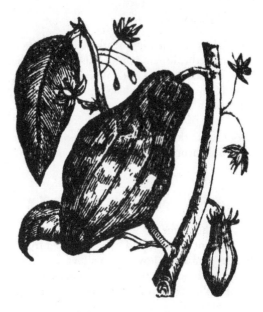

COCOA-BEAN.

Baking Meat

Baking exerts some unexplained influence on meat, rendering it less savoury and less agreeable than meat which has been roasted. 'Those who have travelled in Germany and France,' writes Mr Lewis, one of our most popular scientific authors, 'must have repeatedly marvelled at the singular uniformity in the flavour, or want of flavour, of the various "roasts" served up at the *table d'hôte*.' The general explanation is that the German and French meat is greatly inferior in quality to that of England and Holland, owing to the inferiority of pasturage, and doubtless this is one cause, but it is not the chief cause. The meat is inferior, but the cooking is mainly at fault. The meat is scarcely ever *roasted*, because there is no coal, and firewood is expensive. The meat is therefore *baked*, and the consequence of this baking is that no meat is eatable, or eaten, with its own gravy, but is always accompanied by some sauce more or less piquant.

Weights and Measures

A tablespoonful is frequently mentioned in a recipe, in the prescriptions of medical men and also in medical, chemical and gastronomical works. By it is generally meant and understood a measure or bulk equal to that which would be produced by half an ounce of water.

A dessertspoonful is the half of a tablespoonful; that is to say, by it is meant a measure or bulk equal to a quarter of an ounce of water.

A teaspoonful is equal in quantity to a drachm of water.

A drop: this is the name of a vague kind of measure and is so-called on account of the liquid being dropped from the mouth of a bottle. Its quantity, however, will vary, either from the consistency of the liquid or the size and shape of the mouth of the bottle. The College of Physicians determined the quantity of a drop to be one grain, sixty drops making one fluid drachm. Their drop, or sixtieth part of a fluid drachm, is called a minim.

General Ingredients

Almonds

Almonds are the fruit of the *Amygdalus communis* and are cultivated throughout the whole of the south of Europe, Syria, Persia and Northern Africa, but England is mostly supplied with those which are grown in Spain and the south of France. They are distinguished into sweet and bitter, the produce of different varieties. Of the sweet, there are two varieties, distinguished in commerce by the names of Jordan and Valentia almonds. The former are imported from Malaga and are longer, narrower, more pointed and more highly esteemed than the latter, which are imported from Valentia. Bitter almonds are principally obtained from Morocco and are exported from Mogador.

The almond tree is a native of warmer climates than Britain and is indigenous to the northern parts of Africa and Asia, but it is now commonly cultivated in Italy, Spain and the south of France. It is not usually grown in Britain, and the fruit seldom ripens in this country: it is much admired for the beauty of its blossoms. In the form of its leaves and blossoms, it strongly resembles the peach tree and is included in the same genus by botanists, but the fruit, instead of presenting a delicious pulp like the peach, shrivels up as it ripens and becomes only a tough coriaceous covering to the stone inclosing the eatable kernel, which is surrounded by a thin bitter skin. It flowers early in the spring and produces fruit in August.

Beef

The quality of beef depends on various circumstances, such as the age, the sex, the breed of the animal, and also on the food upon which it has been raised. Bull beef is, in general, dry and tough and by no means possessed of an agreeable flavour; whilst the flesh of the ox is not only highly nourishing and digestible but, if not too old, extremely agreeable. The flesh of the cow is also nourishing, but it is not so agreeable as that of the ox, although that of a heifer is held in high estimation. The flesh of the smaller breeds is much sweeter than that of the larger, which is best when the animal is about seven years old. That of the smaller breeds is best at about five years and that of the cow can hardly be eaten too young.

Butter

Butter is indispensable in almost all culinary preparations. Good fresh butter, used in moderation, is easily digested; it is softening, nutritious and fattening and is far more easily digested than any other of the oleaginous substances sometimes used in its place. About the second century of the Christian era, butter was placed by Galen amongst the useful medical agents, and about a century before him, Dioscorides mentioned that he had noticed that fresh butter, made of ewes' and goats' milk, was served at meals instead of oil and that it took the place of fat in making pastry. Thus we

BUTTER TUB.

have undoubted authority that, eighteen hundred years ago, there existed a knowledge of the useful qualities of butter. The Romans seem to have set about making it much as we do, for Pliny tells us, 'Butter is made from milk, and the use of this aliment, so much sought after by barbarous nations, distinguished the rich from the common people. It is obtained principally from cows' milk; that from ewes is the fattest; goats also supply some. It is produced by agitating the milk in long vessels with narrow openings: a little water is added.'

Butter in Haste: In his *History of Food*, Soyer says that to obtain butter instantly, it is only necessary, in summer, to put new milk into a bottle, some hours after it has been taken from the cow, and shake it briskly. The clots which are thus formed should be thrown into a sieve, washed and pressed together, and they constitute the finest and most delicate butter that can possibly be made.

To Keep and Choose Fresh Butter: Fresh butter should be kept in a dark, cool place and in as large a mass as possible. Mould as much only as is required, as the more surface is exposed, the more liability there will be to spoil and the outside very soon becomes rancid. Fresh butter should be kept covered with white paper. For small larders, butter coolers of red brick are now very much used for keeping fresh butter in warm weather. These coolers are made with a large bell-shaped cover, into the top of which a little cold water should be poured and, in summer time, very frequently changed, and the butter must be kept covered. These coolers keep butter remarkably firm in hot weather and

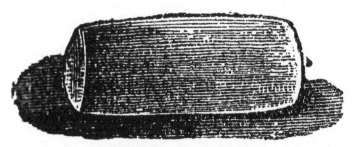

FRESH BUTTER.

are extremely convenient for those whose larder accommodation is limited.

In choosing fresh butter, remember it should smell deliciously and be of an equal colour all through: if it smells sour, it has not been sufficiently washed from the buttermilk, and if veiny and open, it has probably been worked with a staler or an inferior sort.

Another Way to Keep Butter Fresh: One of the best means to preserve butter fresh is, first to completely press out all the buttermilk, then to keep it under water, renewing the water frequently, and to remove it from the influence of heat and air, by wrapping it in a wet cloth.

What to do with Rancid Butter: When butter has become very rancid, it should be melted several times by a moderate heat, with or without the addition of water, and as soon as it has been well kneaded, after the cooling, in order to extract any water it may have retained, it should be put into brown freestone pots, sheltered from the contact of the air. The French often add to it, after it has been melted, a piece of toasted bread, which helps to destroy the tendency of the butter to rancidity.

Beckman, in his *History of Inventions*, states that butter was not used either by the Greeks or Romans in cooking, nor was it brought upon their tables at certain meals, as is the custom at present. In England it has been made from time immemorial, though the art of making cheese is said not to have been known to the ancient Britons, and to have been learned from their conquerors.

The taste of butter is peculiar, and very unlike any other fatty substance. It is extremely agreeable when of the best quality, but its flavour depends much upon the food given to the cows. To be good, it should not adhere to the knife.

Butter, with regard to its dietetic properties, may be regarded nearly in the light of vegetable oils and animal fats, but it becomes sooner rancid than most other fat oils. When fresh, it cannot but be considered as very wholesome, but it should be quite free from rancidity. If slightly salted when it is fresh, its wholesomeness is probably not at all impaired, but should it begin to turn rancid, salting will not correct its unwholesomeness. When salt butter is put into casks, the upper part next the air is very apt to become rancid, and this rancidity is also liable to affect the whole cask.

Epping butter is the kind most esteemed in London. *Fresh butter* comes to London from Buckinghamshire, Suffolk, Oxfordshire, Yorkshire, Devonshire, etc. *Cambridge butter* is esteemed next to fresh; *Devonshire butter* is nearly similar in quality to the latter; *Irish butter* sold in London is all salted but is generally good. The number of firkins exported annually from Ireland amounts to 420,000, equal to a million of money. *Butch butter* is in good repute all over Europe, America and even India, and no country in the world is so successful in the manufacture of this article, Holland supplying more butter to the rest of the world than any country whatever.

There are two methods pursued in the manufacture of butter. In one, the cream is separated from the milk, and in that state it is converted into butter by churning, as is the practice about Epping; in the other, milk is subjected to the same process, which is the method usually followed in Cheshire. The first method is generally said to give the richest butter, and the latter the largest quantity, though some are of opinion that there is little difference either in quality or quantity.

Carbonate of Soda

Soda was called the mineral alkali, because it was originally dug up out of the ground in Africa and other countries: this state of carbonate of soda is called *natron*. But carbonate of soda is likewise procured from the combustion of marine plants, or such as grow on the sea shore. Pure carbonate of soda is employed for making effervescing draughts, with lemon juice, citric acid or tartaric acid. The chief constituent of soda, the alkali, has been used in France from time immemorial in the manufacture of soap and glass, two chemical productions which employ and keep in circulation an immense amount of capital. A small pinch of carbonate of soda will give an extraordinary lightness to puff pastes and, introduced into the teapot, will extract the full strength of the tea. But its qualities have a powerful effect upon delicate constitutions, and it is not to be used incautiously in any preparation.

TEAPOT.

Currants

The utility of currants, red, black or white, has long been established in domestic economy. The juice of the red species,

CURRANTS.

if boiled with an equal weight of loaf sugar, forms an agreeable substance called currant jelly, much employed in sauces and very valuable in the cure of sore throats and colds. The French mix it with sugar and water and thus form an agreeable beverage. The juice of currants is a valuable remedy in obstructions of the bowels; and, in complaints, it is useful on account of its readily quenching thirst and for its cooling effect on the stomach. White- and flesh-coloured currants have, with the exception of flavour, in every respect, the same qualities as the red species. Both white and red currants are pleasant additions to the dessert, but the black variety is mostly used for culinary and medicinal purposes, especially in the form of jelly for quinsies. The leaves of the black currant make a pleasant tea.

Zante Currants: The dried fruit which goes by the name of currants in grocers' shops is not a currant really but a small kind of grape, chiefly cultivated in the Morea and the Ionian Islands, Corfu, Zante, etc. Those of Zante are cultivated in an immense plain, under the shelter of mountains, on the shore of the island, where the sun has great power and brings them to maturity. When gathered

ZANTE CURRANTS.

and dried by the sun and air, on mats, they are conveyed to magazines, heaped together, and left to cake, until ready for shipping. They are then dug out by iron crowbars, trodden into casks and exported. The fertile vale of 'Zante the woody' produces about 9,000,000 lbs of currants annually. In cakes and puddings, this delicious little grape is most extensively used; in fact, we could not make a plum pudding without the currant.

Eggs

There is only one opinion as to the nutritive properties of eggs, although the qualities of those belonging to different birds vary somewhat. Those of the common hen are most esteemed as delicate food, particularly when 'new-laid'. The quality of eggs depends much upon the food given to the hen. Eggs in general are considered most easily digestible when little subjected to the art of cookery. The lightest way of dressing them is by poaching, which is effected by putting them for a minute or two into brisk boiling water: this coagulates the external white, without doing the inner part too much. Eggs are much better when new-laid than a day or two afterwards. The usual time allotted for boiling eggs in the shell is 3 to 3¾ minutes; less time than that in boiling water will not be sufficient to solidify the white and more will make the yolk hard and less digestible: it is very difficult to guess accurately as to the time. Great care should be employed in putting them into the water, to prevent cracking the shell, which inevitably causes a portion of the white to exude and lets water into the egg. Eggs are often beaten up raw in nutritive beverages.

Eggs are employed in a very great many articles of cookery, entries and entremets, and they form an essential ingredient in pastry, creams, flip, etc. It is particularly necessary that they should be quite fresh, as nothing is worse than stale eggs. Cobbett justly says stale or even preserved eggs are things to be run from, not after.

The Metropolis is supplied with eggs from all parts of the kingdom, and they are likewise largely imported from various places on the continent as France, Holland, Belgium, Guernsey and Jersey. It appears from official statements mentioned in McCulloch's *Commercial Dictionary* that the number imported from France alone amounts to about 60,000,000 a year, and supposing them on an average to cost fourpence a dozen, it follows that we pay our continental neighbours above £83,000 a year for eggs.

The eggs of different birds vary much in size and colour. Those of the ostrich are the largest: one laid in the menagerie in Paris weighed 2 lbs 14 oz, held a pint and was 6 inches deep: this is about the usual size of those brought from Africa. Travellers describe ostrich eggs as of an agreeable taste: they keep longer than hens' eggs. Drinking cups are often made of the shell, which is very strong. The eggs of the turkey are almost as mild as those of the hen; the egg of the goose is large but well tasting. Duck's eggs have a rich flavour; the albumen is slightly transparent, or bluish, when set or coagulated by boiling, which requires less time than hens' eggs. Guinea fowl eggs are smaller and more delicate than those of the hen. Eggs of wildfowl are generally coloured, often spotted, and the taste generally partakes

HENS' EGGS.

somewhat of the flavour of the bird they belong to. Those of land birds that are eaten, as the plover lapwing, ruffy, etc., are in general much esteemed, but those of sea fowl have, more or less, a strong fishy taste. The eggs of the turtle are very numerous: they consist of yolk only, without shell, and are delicious.

Eggs contain, for their volume, a greater quantity of nutriment than any other article of food. But it does not follow that they are always good for weak stomachs; quite the contrary, for it is often a great object to give the stomach a large surface to work upon, a considerable volume of *ingesta*, over which the nutritive matter is diffused, and so exposed to the action of the gastric juice at many points. There are many persons who cannot digest eggs, however cooked. It is said, however, that their digestibility decreases in proportion to the degree in which they are hardened by boiling.

To Choose Eggs: Hold them before a lighted candle, or to the light, and if the egg looks clear, it will be tolerably good; if thick, it is stale, and if there is a black spot attached to the shell, it is worthless. No egg should be used for culinary purposes with the slightest taint in it, as it will render perfectly useless those with which it has been mixed. Eggs that are purchased, and that cannot be relied on, should always be broken in a cup and then put into a basin: by this means, stale or bad eggs may be easily rejected, without wasting the others.

Flour

Nutritious Qualities: The gluten of grain and the albumen of vegetable juices are identical in composition with the albumen of blood. Vegetable casein has also the composition of animal caseine. The finest wheat flour contains more starch than the coarser; the bran of wheat is proportionably richer in gluten. Rye and rye bread contain a substance resembling starch gum (or dextrine, as it is called) in its properties, which is very easily converted into sugar. The starch of barley approaches in many properties to cellulose and is, therefore, less digestible. Oats are particularly rich in plastic substances; Scotch oats are richer than those grown in England or in Germany. Fine American flour is one of the varieties which is richest in gluten and is consequently one of the most nutritious.

Lobster

This is one of the crab tribe and is found on most of the rocky coasts of Great Britain. Some are caught with the hand, but the larger number in pots, which serve all the purposes of a trap, being made of osiers and baited with garbage. They are shaped like a wire mousetrap, so that when the lobsters once enter them, they cannot get out again. They are fastened to a cord and sunk in the sea, and their place marked by a buoy. The fish is very prolific, and deposits its eggs in the sand, where they are soon hatched. On the coast of Norway, they are very abundant, and it is from there that the English metropolis is mostly supplied. They are rather indigestible and, as a food, not so nutritive as they are supposed to be.

Macaroni

Macaroni is composed of wheaten flour, flavoured with other articles, and worked up with water into a paste, to which, by a peculiar process, a tubular or pipe form is given, in order that it may cook more readily in hot water. That of smaller diameter than macaroni (which is about the thickness of a goose quill) is called vermicelli, and when smaller still, fidelini. The finest is made from the flour of the hard-grained Black Sea wheat. Macaroni is the principal article of food in many parts of Italy,

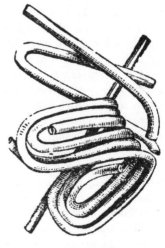

MACARONI.

particularly Naples, where the best is manufactured, and from whence, also, it is exported in considerable quantities. In this country, macaroni and vermicelli are frequently used in soups.

Manna Kroup, Semora or Semolina

These are three names given to a flour made from ground wheat and rice. The preparation is white when it is made only of these materials; the yellow colour, which it usually has, is produced by a portion of saffron and yolks of eggs. Next to vermicelli, this preparation is the most useful for thickening either meat or vegetable soups. As a food, it is light, nutritious, wholesome and easily digested. The best preparation is brought from Arabia and, next to that, from Italy.

Milk

Milk is obtained only from the class of animals called *Mammalia* and is intended by Nature for the nourishment of their young.

The milk of each animal is distinguished by some peculiarities, but as that of the cow is by far the most useful to us in this part of the world, our observations will be confined to that variety.

Milk, when drawn from the cow, is of a yellowish white colour and is the most yellow at the beginning of the period of lactation. Its taste is agreeable and rather saccharine. The viscidity and specific gravity of milk are somewhat greater than that of water, but these properties vary somewhat in the milk procured from different individuals. On an average, the specific gravity of milk is 1.035, water being 1. The small cows of the Alderney breed afford the richest milk.

Milk which is carried to a considerable distance, so as to be much agitated, and cooled before it is put into pans to settle for cream, never throws up so much, nor such rich cream, as if the same milk had been put into pans directly after it was milked.

Milk, considered as an aliment, is of such importance in domestic economy as to render all the improvements in its production extremely valuable. To enlarge upon the antiquity of its use is unnecessary; it has always been a favourite food in Britain. 'Laete et carne vivunt', says Caesar, in his *Commentaries*; the English of which is, 'the inhabitants subsist upon flesh and milk'. The breed of the cow has received great improvement in modern times, as regards the quantity and quality of the milk which she affords; the form of milch cows, their mode of nourishment and progress are also manifest in the management of the dairy.

Although milk in its natural state be a fluid; yet, considered as an aliment, it is both solid and fluid: For no sooner does it enter the stomach, than it is coagulated by the gastric juice, and separated into curd and whey, the first of these being extremely nutritive.

From no other substance, solid or fluid, can so great a number of distinct kinds of aliment be prepared as from milk; some forming food, others drink; some of them delicious and deserving the name of luxuries; all of them wholesome, and some medicinal: indeed, the variety of aliments that seems capable of being produced from milk, appears to be quite endless. In every age, this must have been a subject for experiment, and every nation has added to the number by the invention of some peculiarity of its own.

If it be desired that the milk should be freed entirely from cream, it should be poured into a very shallow broad pan or dish, not more than 1½ inches deep, so that the cream has not to rise through a great depth of milk. In cold and wet weather, milk is not so rich as it is in summer and warm weather, and the morning's milk is always richer than the evening's. The last-drawn milk of each milking, at all times and seasons, is richer than the first drawn, and on that account should be set apart for cream. Milk should be shaken as little as possible when carried from the cow to the dairy and should be poured into the pans very gently. Persons not keeping cows may always have a little cream, provided the milk they purchase be pure and unadulterated. As soon as it comes in, it should be poured into very shallow open pie dishes, and set by in a very cool place, and in 7 or 8 hours, a nice cream should have risen to the surface.

Milk, when of good quality, is of an opaque white colour: the cream always comes to the top; the well-known milky odour is strong; it will boil without altering its appearance, in these respects; the little bladders which arise on the surface will renew themselves if broken by the spoon. To boil milk is, in fact, the simplest way of testing its quality. The commonest adulterations of milk are not of a hurtful character. It is a good deal thinned with water, and sometimes thickened with a little starch, or coloured with yolk of egg, or even saffron, but these processes have nothing murderous in them.

Pigeon

The pigeon tribe forms a connecting link between the passerine birds and poultry. They are widely distributed over the world, some of the species being found even in the arctic regions. Their chief food is grain, and they drink much; not at intervals, like other birds, but by a continuous draught, like quadrupeds. The wild pigeon, or stock dove, is the parent whence all the varieties of the domestic pigeon are derived. In the wild state, it is still found in many parts of this island, making its nest in the holes of rocks, in the hollows of trees or in old towers but never, like the ringdove, on branches. The blue house pigeon is the variety principally reared for the table in this country and is produced from our farmyards in great numbers. When young, and still fed by their parents, they are most preferable for the table and are called *squabs*; under six months, they are denominated *squeakers*, and at six months, they begin to breed. Their flesh is accounted savoury, delicate and stimulating, and the dark-coloured birds are considered to have the highest flavour, while the light are esteemed to have the more delicate flesh.

Potato

The potato belongs to the family of the *Solanaceae*, the greater number of which inhabit the tropics, and the remainder are distributed over the temperate regions of both hemispheres but do not extend to the arctic and antarctic zones. The whole of the family are auspicious; a great number are narcotic, and many are deleterious. The roots partake of the properties of the plants and are sometimes even more active. The tubercles of such as produce them are amylaceous and nutritive, as in those of the potato. The leaves are generally narcotic, but they lose this principle in boiling, as is the case with the *solanum nigrum*, which are used as a vegetable when cooked.

Raisins

Raisins are grapes, prepared by suffering them to remain on the vine until they are perfectly ripe and then drying them in the sun or by the heat of an oven. The sun-dried grapes are sweet, the oven-dried of an acid flavour. The common way of drying grapes for raisins is to tie two or three bunches of them together, whilst yet on the vine, and dip them into a hot lixivium of wood ashes mixed with a little of the oil of olives: this disposes them shrink and wrinkle, after which they are left on the vine for three or four days, separated on sticks in a horizontal situation and then dried in the sun at leisure, after being cut from the tree.

Rice

Rice, with the proper management in cooking it, forms a very valuable and cheap addition to our farinaceous food and, in years of scarcity, has been found eminently useful in lessening the consumption of flour. When boiled, it should be so managed that the grains, though soft, should be as little broken and as dry as possible. The water in which it is dressed should only simmer, and not boil hard. Very little water should be used, as the grains absorb a great deal and, consequently, swell much; and if they take up too much at first, it is difficult to get rid of it. Baking it in puddings is the best mode of preparing it.

Varieties of Rice: Of the varieties of rice brought to our market, that from Bengal is chiefly of the species denominated *cargo* rice and is of a coarse reddish brown cast but peculiarly sweet and large grained; it does not readily separate from the husk, but it is preferred by the natives to all the others. *Patna* rice is more esteemed in Europe and is of very superior quality; it is small grained, rather long and wiry, and is remarkably white. The *Carolina* rice is considered as the best and is likewise the dearest in London.

EARS OF RICE.

Sago

Sago is the pith of a species of palm (*Cycas circinalis*). Its form is that of a small round grain. There are two sorts of sago: the white and the yellow, but their properties are the same. Sago absorbs

SAGO PALM.

the liquid in which it is cooked, becomes transparent and soft and retains its original shape. Its alimentary properties are the same as those of tapioca and arrowroot.

Semolina

After vermicelli, semolina is the most useful ingredient that can be used for thickening soups, meat or vegetable, of rich or simple quality. Semolina is softening, light, wholesome, easy of digestion and adapted to the infant, the aged and the invalid. That of a clear yellow colour, well dried and newly made, is the fittest for use.

Sugar

Sugar has been happily called 'the honey of reeds'. The sugar cane appears to be originally a native of the East Indies. The Chinese have cultivated it for 2,000 years. The Egyptians,

Phoenicians and Jews knew nothing about it. The Greek physicians are the first who speak of it. It was not till the year 1471 that a Venetian discovered the method of purifying brown sugar and making loaf sugar. He gained an immense fortune by this discovery. Our supplies are now obtained from Barbados, Jamaica, Mauritius, Ceylon, the East and West Indies generally and the United States, but the largest supplies come from Cuba. Sugar is divided into the following classes: refined sugar, white clayed, brown clayed, brown raw and molasses. The sugar cane grows to the height of 6, 12 or even sometimes 20 feet. It is propagated from cuttings, requires much hoeing and weeding, and attains maturity in twelve or thirteen months. When ripe, it is cut down close to the stole, the stems are divided into lengths of about 3 feet, which are made up into bundles, and carried to the mill to be crushed between rollers. In the process of crushing, the juice runs down into a reservoir, from which, after a while, it is drawn through a siphon; that is to say, the clear fluid is taken from the scum. This fluid undergoes several processes of drying and refining; the methods varying in different manufactories. There are some large establishments engaged in sugar refining in the neighbourhoods of Blackwall and Bethnal Green, London. The process is mostly in the hands of German workmen. Sugar is adulterated with fine sand and sawdust. Pure sugar is highly nutritious, adding to the fatty tissue of the body, but it is not easy of digestion.

Introduction of sugar: Sugar was first known as a drug, and used by the apothecaries, and with them was a most important article. At its first appearance, some said it was heating; others, that it injured the chest; others, that it disposed persons to apoplexy; the truth, however, soon conquered these fancies and the use of sugar has increased every day, and there is no household in the civilised world which can do without it.

Tapioca

Tapioca is recommended to the convalescent, as being easy of digestion. It may be used in soup or broth, or mixed with milk or water, and butter. It is excellent food for either the healthy or sick, for the reason that it is so quickly digested without fatigue to the stomach.

Treacle or Molasses

Treacle is the uncrystallisable part of the saccharine juice drained from the muscovado sugar, and it is either naturally so or rendered uncrystallisable through some defect in the process of boiling. As it contains a large quantity of sweet or saccharine principle and is cheap, it is of great use as an article of domestic economy. Children are especially fond of it, and it is accounted wholesome. It is also useful for making beer, rum and the very dark syrups.

Vanilla

Vanille, or Vanilla, is the fruit of the *vanillier*, a parasitical herbaceous plant, which flourishes in Brazil, Mexico, and Peru. The fruit is a long capsule, thick and fleshy. Certain species of this fruit contain a pulp with a delicious perfume and flavour. Vanilla is principally imported from Mexico. The capsules for export are always picked at perfect maturity. The essence is the form in which it is used generally and most conveniently. Its properties are stimulating and exciting. It is in daily use for ices, chocolates, and flavouring confections generally.

Yeast

Yeast consists principally of a substance very similar in composition, and in many of its sensible properties, to gluten, and, when new or fresh, it is inflated and rendered frothy by a large quantity of carbonic acid. When mixed with wort, this substance acts upon the saccharine matter; the temperature rises, carbonic acid is disengaged and the result is ale, which always contains a considerable proportion of alcohol or spirit. The quantity of yeast employed in brewing ale being small, the saccharine matter is but imperfectly decomposed: hence a considerable portion of it remains in the liquor and gives it that viscid quality and body for which it is remarkable. The fermenting property of yeast is weakened by boiling for 10 minutes and is entirely destroyed by continuing the boiling. Alcohol poured upon it likewise renders it inert; on which account its power lessens as the alcohol is formed during fermentation.

Recipes for All Year Round

Biscuits

Arrowroot Biscuits or Drops

Ingredients

½ lb of butter
6 eggs
½ lb of flour
6 oz of arrowroot
½ lb of pounded loaf sugar

Mode

Beat the butter to a cream; whisk the eggs to a strong froth, add
them to the butter, stir in the flour a little at a time, and beat the

ARROWROOT.

mixture well. Break down all the lumps from the arrowroot and add that, with the sugar, to the other ingredients. Mix all well together, drop the dough on a buttered tin in pieces the size of a shilling, and bake the biscuits about ¼ hour in a slow oven.

Time

¼ hour.
Sufficient to make from three to four dozen biscuits.

Cocoanut Biscuits or Cakes

Ingredients

10 oz of sifted sugar
3 eggs
6 oz of grated cocoa-nut

Mode

Whisk the eggs until they are very light; add the sugar gradually; then stir in the cocoanut. Roll a tablespoonful of the paste at a time in your hands in the form of a pyramid; place the pyramids on paper, put the paper on tins and bake the biscuits in rather a cool oven until they are just coloured a light brown.

Time

About ¼ hour.

Crisp Biscuits

Ingredients

1 lb of flour
The yolk of 1 egg
Milk

Mode

Mix the flour and the yolk of the egg with sufficient milk to make the whole into a very stiff paste, beat it well and knead it until it is perfectly smooth. Roll the paste out very thin; with a round cutter shape it into small biscuits and bake them a nice brown in a slow oven from 12 to 18 minutes.

Time

12 to 18 minutes.

Dessert Biscuits, which may be flavoured with ground ginger, cinnamon, etc.

Ingredients

1 lb of flour
½ lb of butter
½ lb of sifted sugar
The yolks of 6 eggs
Flavouring to taste

Mode

Put the butter into a basin; warm it, but do not allow it to oil, then with the hand beat it to a cream. Add the flour by degrees, then the sugar and flavouring, and moisten the whole with the yolks of the eggs, which should previously be well beaten. When all the ingredients are thoroughly incorporated, drop the mixture from a spoon onto a buttered paper, leaving a distance between each cake, as they spread as soon as they begin to get warm. Bake in rather a slow oven from 12 to 18 minutes and do not let the biscuits acquire too much colour. In making the above quantity, half may be flavoured with ground ginger and the other half with essence of lemon or currants to make a variety. With whatever the preparation is flavoured, so are the biscuits called, and an endless variety may be made in this manner.

Time

12 to 18 minutes, or rather longer, in a very slow oven.
Sufficient to make from three to four dozen cakes.

Geneva Wafers

Ingredients

2 eggs
3 oz of butter
3 oz of flour
3 oz of pounded sugar

Mode

Well whisk the eggs; put them into a basin, and stir to them the butter, which should be beaten to a cream; add the flour and sifted sugar gradually and then mix all well together. Butter a baking sheet and drop on it a teaspoonful of the mixture at a time, leaving a space between each. Bake in a cool oven; watch the pieces of paste, and, when half done, roll them up like wafers and put in a small wedge of bread or piece of wood, to keep them in shape. Return them to the oven until crisp. Before serving, remove the bread, put a spoonful of preserve in the widest end and fill up with whipped cream. This is a very pretty and ornamental dish for the supper table, and is very nice and very easily made.

Time

Altogether 20 to 25 minutes.
Sufficient for a nice-sized dish.

Lemon Biscuits

Ingredients

1¼ lbs of flour
¾ lb of loaf sugar
6 oz of fresh butter
4 eggs
1 oz of lemon peel
2 dessertspoonfuls of lemon juice

Mode

Rub the flour into the butter; stir in the pounded sugar and very finely minced lemon peel, and when these ingredients are thoroughly mixed, add the eggs, which should be previously well whisked, and the lemon juice. Beat the mixture well for a minute or two, then drop it from a spoon on to a buttered tin, about two inches apart, as the cakes will spread when they get warm; place the tin in the oven and bake the cakes of a pale brown for 15 to 20 minutes.

Time

15 to 20 minutes.

Macaroons

Ingredients

½ lb of sweet almonds
½ lb of sifted loaf sugar
The whites of 3 eggs
Wafer paper

Mode

Blanch, skin and dry the almonds and pound them well with a little orange flower water or plain water, then add to them the sifted sugar and the whites of the eggs, which should be beaten to a stiff froth, and mix all the ingredients well together. When the paste looks soft, drop it at equal distances from a biscuit syringe on to sheets of wafer paper; put a strip of almond on the top of

MACAROONS.

each; strew some sugar over and bake the macaroons in rather a slow oven, of a light brown colour. When hard and set, they are done, and must not be allowed to get very brown, as that would spoil their appearance. If the cakes, when baked, appear heavy, add a little more white of egg [next time], but let this always be whisked before it is added to the other ingredients. We have given a recipe for making these cakes, but we think it almost or quite as economical to purchase articles such as these at a good confectioner's.

Time

From 15 to 20 minutes, in a slow oven.

Ratafias

Ingredients

¾ lb of sweet almonds
¾ lb of sifted loaf sugar
The whites of 4 eggs.

Mode

Blanch, skin and dry the almonds and pound them in a mortar with the white of an egg; stir in the sugar and gradually add the remaining whites of eggs, taking care that they are very

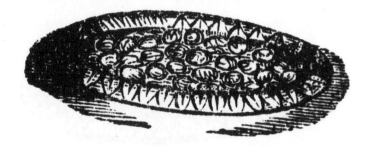

RATAFIAS.

thoroughly whisked. Drop the mixture through a small biscuit syringe on to cartridge paper* and bake the cakes for 10 to 12 minutes in rather a quicker oven than for macaroons. A very small quantity should be dropped on the paper to form one cake, as when baked, the ratafias should be about the size of a large button.

Time

10 to 12 minutes.
*[N.B. Do not use cartridge paper for baking purposes.]

Rice Biscuits or Cakes

Ingredients

To every ½ lb of rice flour allow ¼ lb of pounded lump sugar, ¼ lb of butter, 2 eggs.

Mode

Beat the butter to a cream, stir in the rice flour and pounded sugar and moisten the whole with the eggs, which should be previously well beaten. Roll out the paste, shape it with a round

SMALL CAKES FOR TEA.

pastry cutter into small cakes and bake them for 12 to 18 minutes in a very slow oven.

Time

12 to 18 minutes.
Sufficient to make about eighteen cakes.

Rock Biscuits

Ingredients

6 eggs
1 lb of sifted sugar
½ lb of flour
A few currants

Mode

Break the eggs into a basin, beat them well until very light, add the pounded sugar and when this is well mixed with the eggs, dredge in the flour gradually and add the currants. Mix all well together and put the dough, with a fork, on the tins, making it look as rough as possible. Bake the cakes in a moderate oven from 20 minutes to half an hour; when they are done, allow them to get cool and store them away in a tin canister, in a dry place.

Time

20 minutes to ½ hour.

Savoy Biscuits or Cakes

Ingredients

4 eggs
6 oz of pounded sugar
The rind of 1 lemon
6 oz of flour

Mode

Break the eggs into a basin, separating the whites from the yolks; beat the yolks well, mix with them the pounded sugar and grated lemon rind, and beat these ingredients together for about a quarter of an hour. Then dredge in the flour gradually, and when the whites of the eggs have been whisked to a solid froth, stir them to the flour, etc.; beat the mixture well for another 5 minutes, then draw it along in strips upon thick cartridge paper* to the proper size of the biscuit and bake them in rather a hot oven, but let them be carefully watched, as they are soon done, and a few seconds over the proper time will scorch and spoil them. These biscuits, or ladies' fingers, as they are called, are used for making Charlotte Russes and for a variety of fancy sweet dishes.

Time

5 to 8 minutes, in a quick oven.
*[N.B. Do not use cartridge paper for baking purposes.]

Scotch Shortbread

Ingredients

2 lbs of flour
1 lb of butter
¼ lb of pounded loaf sugar
½ oz of caraway seeds
1 oz of sweet almonds
A few strips of candied orange peel

Mode

Beat the butter to a cream, gradually dredge in the flour, and add the sugar, caraway seeds, and sweet almonds, which should be blanched and cut into small pieces. Work the paste until it is quite smooth, and divide it into six pieces. Put each cake on a separate piece of paper, roll the paste out square to the thickness of about an inch, and pinch it upon all sides. Prick it well, and ornament with one or two strips of candied orange peel. Put the cakes into a good oven, and bake them from 25 to 30 minutes.

SHORTBREAD.

Time

25 to 30 minutes.
Sufficient to make six cakes.
Note: Where the flavour of the caraway seeds is disliked, omit them, and add rather a larger proportion of candied peel.

Seed Biscuits

Ingredients

1 lb of flour
¼ lb of sifted sugar
¼ lb of butter
½ oz of caraway seeds
3 eggs

Mode

Beat the butter to a cream; stir in the flour, sugar and caraway seeds, and when these ingredients are well mixed, add the eggs, which should be well whisked. Roll out the paste, with a round cutter shape out the biscuits, and bake them in a moderate oven for 10 to 15 minutes. The tops of the biscuits may be brushed over with a little milk or the white of an egg, and then a little sugar strewn over.

Time

10 to 15 minutes.
Sufficient to make three dozen biscuits.

Simple Hard Biscuits

Ingredients

To every lb of flour allow 2 oz of butter and about ½ pint of skimmed milk.

Mode

Warm the butter in the milk until the former is dissolved and then mix it with the flour into a very stiff paste; beat it with a rolling pin until the dough looks perfectly smooth. Roll it out thin; cut it with the top of a glass into round biscuits; prick them well and bake them for 6 to 10 minutes. The above is the proportion of milk which we think would convert the flour into a stiff paste; but should it be found to be too much, an extra spoonful or two of flour must be put in. These biscuits are very nice for the cheese course.

Time

6 to 10 minutes.

Soda Biscuits

Ingredients

1 lb of flour
½ lb of pounded loaf sugar
¼ lb of fresh butter
2 eggs
1 small teaspoonful of carbonate of soda

Mode

Put the flour (which should be perfectly dry) into a basin; rub in the butter, add the sugar and mix these ingredients well together. Whisk the eggs, stir them into the mixture and beat it well, until everything is well incorporated. Quickly stir in the soda, roll the paste out until it is about half an inch thick, cut it into small round cakes with a tin cutter and bake them for 12 to 18 minutes

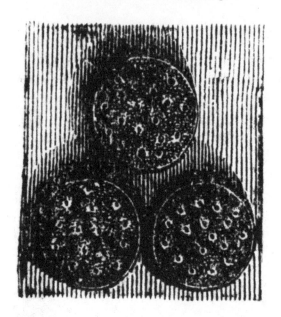

SODA BISCUITS.

in rather a brisk oven. After the soda is added, great expedition is necessary in rolling and cutting out the paste and in putting the biscuits *immediately* into the oven, or they will be heavy.

Time

12 to 18 minutes.
Sufficient to make about three dozen cakes.

Bread

Yeast

To Make Yeast for Bread

Ingredients

1½ oz of hops
3 quarts of water

1 lb of bruised malt
½ pint of yeast

Mode

Boil the hops in the water for 20 minutes; let it stand for about 5 minutes, then add it to 1 lb of bruised malt prepared as for brewing. Let the mixture stand covered till about lukewarm; then put in not quite half a pint of yeast; keep it warm, and let it work 3 or 4 hours; then put it into small half-pint bottles (ginger-beer bottles are the best for the purpose), cork them well, and tie them down. The yeast is now ready for use; it will keep good for a few weeks, and one bottle will be found sufficient for 18 lbs of flour. When required for use, boil 3 lbs of potatoes without salt, mash them in the same water in which they were boiled, and rub through a colander. Stir in about ½ lb of flour; then put in the yeast, pour it into the middle of the flour, and let it stand warm on the hearth all night, and in the morning let it be quite warm when it is kneaded. The bottles of yeast require very careful opening, as it is generally exceedingly ripe.

Time

20 minutes to boil the hops and water, the yeast to work 3 or 4 hours.

Sufficient

½ pint sufficient for 18 lbs of flour.

Kirkleatham Yeast

Ingredients

2 oz of hops
4 quarts of water
½ lb of flour
½ pint of yeast

Mode

Boil the hops and water for 20 minutes; strain, and mix with the liquid ½ lb of flour and not quite ½ pint of yeast. Bottle it up and tie the corks down. When wanted for use, boil potatoes according to the quantity of bread to be made (about 3 lbs are sufficient for about a peck of flour); mash them, add to them ½ lb of flour and mix about ½ pint of the yeast with them; let this mixture stand all day, and lay the bread to rise the night before it is wanted.

Time

20 minutes to boil the hops and water.

Sufficient

½ pint of this yeast is sufficient for a peck of flour, or rather more.

To Make Good Home-Made Bread
(Miss Acton's recipe)

Ingredients

1 quartern of flour
1 large tablespoonful of solid brewer's yeast, or nearly 1 oz of fresh German yeast
1¼ to 1½ pints of warm milk and water

Mode

Put the flour into a large earthenware bowl or deep pan; then with a strong metal or wooden spoon, hollow out the middle, but do not clear it entirely away from the bottom of the pan, as, in that case, the sponge (or leaven, as it was formerly termed) would stick to it, which it ought not to do. Next, take either a large tablespoonful of brewer's yeast which has been rendered solid by mixing it with plenty of cold water and letting it afterwards stand to settle for a day and night, or nearly an ounce of German yeast; put it into a large basin, and proceed to mix it, so that it shall be as smooth as cream, with ¾ pint of warm milk and water or with water only; though even a very little milk will much improve the bread. Pour the yeast into the hole made in the flour and stir into it as much of that which lies round it as will make a thick batter, in which there must be no lumps. Strew plenty of flour on the top; throw a thick clean cloth over and set it where the air is warm, but do not place it upon the kitchen fender, for it will become too much heated there. Look at it from time to time: when it has been laid for nearly an hour and when the yeast has risen and broken through the flour, so that bubbles appear in it, you will know that it is ready to be made up into dough. Then place the plan on a strong chair, or dresser, or table, of convenient height; pour into the sponge the remainder of the warm milk and water; stir into it as much of the flour as you can with the spoon, then wipe it out clean with your fingers and lay it aside. Next take plenty of the remaining flour, throw it on the top of the leaven and begin, with the knuckles of both hands, to knead it well. When the flour is nearly all kneaded in, begin to draw the edges of the dough towards the middle, in order to mix the whole thoroughly, and when it is free from flour and lumps and crumbs, and does not stick to the hands when touched, it will be done and may again be covered with the cloth and left to rise a second time. In ¾ hour look at it, and should it have swollen very much, and begin to crack, it will be light enough to bake. Turn it then on to a paste board or very clean dresser, and with a large sharp knife divide it in two; make it up quickly into loaves and dispatch it to the oven: make one or two incisions across the tops of the loaves, as they will rise more easily if this be done. If baked in tins or pans, rub them with a tiny piece of butter laid on a piece of clean paper to prevent the dough from sticking to them. All bread should be turned upside down, or on its side, as it is drawn from the oven: if this be neglected, the under part of the loaves will become wet and blistered from the steam, which cannot then escape from them. To make the dough without setting a sponge, merely mix the yeast with the greater part of the warm milk and water and wet up the whole of the flour at once after a little salt has been stirred in, proceeding exactly, in every other respect, as in the directions just given. As the dough will *soften* in the rising, it should be made quite firm at first or it will be too lithe by the time it is ready for the oven.

Time

To be left to rise an hour the first time, ¾ hour the second time; to be baked from 1 to 1¼ hours or baked in one loaf from 1½ to 2 hours.

To Make a Peck of Good Bread

Ingredients

3 lbs of potatoes
6 pints of cold water
½ pint of good yeast
A peck of flour
2 oz of salt

Mode

Peel and boil the potatoes; beat them to a cream while warm, then add a pint of cold water, strain through a colander and add to it ½ pint of good yeast, which should have been put in water overnight to take off its bitterness. Stir all well together with a wooden spoon and pour the mixture into the centre of the flour; mix it to the substance of cream, cover it over closely and let it remain near the fire for an hour, then add the 5 pints of water, milk-warm, with 2 oz of salt; pour this in and mix the whole to a nice light dough. Let it remain for about 2 hours, then make it into seven loaves and bake for about 1½ hours in a good oven. When baked, the bread should weigh nearly 20 lbs.

Time

About 1½ hours.

Indian Corn Flour Bread

Ingredients

To 4 lbs of flour allow 2 lbs of Indian Corn flour, 2 tablespoonfuls of yeast, 3 pints of warm water, ¼ oz of salt.

Mode

Mix the two flours well together, with the salt; make a hole in the centre, and stir the yeast up well with ½ pint of the warm water; put this into the middle of the flour and mix enough of it with the yeast to make a thin batter; throw a little flour over the surface of this batter, cover the whole with a thick cloth and set it to rise in a warm place. When the batter has nicely risen, work the whole to a nice smooth dough, adding the water as required; knead it well and mould the dough into loaves; let them rise for nearly ½ hour, then put them into a well-heated oven. If made into two loaves, they will require from 1½ to 2 hours' baking.

Time

1½ to 2 hours.

Rice Bread

Ingredients

To every lb of rice allow 4 lbs of wheat flour, nearly 3 tablespoonfuls of yeast, ¼ oz of salt.

Mode

Boil the rice in water until it is quite tender; pour off the water and put the rice, before it is cold, into the flour. Mix these well together with the yeast, salt and sufficient warm water to make the whole into a smooth dough. Let it rise by the side of the fire, then form it into loaves and bake them from 1½ to 2 hours, according to their size. If the rice is boiled in milk instead of water, it makes very delicious bread or cakes. When boiled in this manner, it may be mixed with the flour without straining the liquid from it.

Time

1½ to 2 hours.

Excellent Rolls

Ingredients

To every lb of flour allow 1 oz of butter, ¼ pint of milk, 1 large teaspoonful of yeast, a little salt.

ROLLS.

Mode

Warm the butter in the milk, add to it the yeast and salt and mix these ingredients well together. Put the flour into a pan, stir in the above ingredients and let the dough rise, covered, in a warm place. Knead it well, make it into rolls, let them rise again for a few minutes and bake in a quick oven. Richer rolls may be made by adding one or two eggs and a larger proportion of butter, and their appearance improved by brushing the tops over with yolk of egg or a little milk.

Time

1 lb of flour, divided into 6 rolls, from 15 to 20 minutes.

Hot Rolls

This dish, although very unwholesome and indigestible, is nevertheless eaten by many persons. As soon as the rolls come from the baker's, they should be put into the oven, which, in the early part of the morning, is sure not to be very hot, and the rolls must not be buttered until wanted. When they are quite hot, divide them lengthwise into three; put some thin flakes of good butter between the slices, press the rolls together and put them in the oven for a minute or two, but not longer, or the butter would oil. Take them out of the oven, spread the butter equally over, divide the rolls in half, put them on to a very hot clean dish and send them instantly to table.

Soda Bread

Ingredients

To every 2 lbs of flour allow 1 teaspoonful of tartaric acid, 1 teaspoonful of salt, 1 teaspoonful of carbonate of soda, 2 breakfast cupfuls of cold milk.

Mode

Let the tartaric acid and salt be reduced to the finest possible powder, then mix them well with the flour. Dissolve the soda in the milk and pour it several times from one basin to another, before adding it to the flour. Work the whole quickly into a light dough, divide it into two loaves, put them into a well-heated oven immediately and bake for an hour. Sour milk or buttermilk may be used, but then a little less acid will be needed.

Time

1 hour.

To Make Dry Toast

To make dry toast properly, a great deal of attention is required; much more, indeed, than people generally suppose. Never use new bread for making any kind of toast, as it eats heavy and, besides, is very extravagant. Procure a loaf of household bread about two days old; cut off as many slices as may be required, not quite ¼ inch in thickness; trim off the crusts and ragged edges, put the bread on a toasting fork and hold it before a very clear fire. Move it backwards and forwards until the bread is nicely coloured; then turn it and toast the other side and do not place it so near the fire that it blackens. Dry toast should be more gradually made than buttered toast, as its great beauty consists in its crispness and this cannot be attained unless the process is slow and the bread is allowed gradually to colour. It should never be made long before it is wanted, as it soon becomes tough, unless placed on the fender in front of the fire. As soon as each piece is ready, it should be put into a rack, or stood upon its edges, and sent quickly to table.

To Make Hot Buttered Toast

A loaf of household bread about two days old answers for making toast better than cottage bread, the latter not being a good shape, and too crusty for purpose. Cut as many nice even slices as may be required, rather more than ¼ inch in thickness, and toast them before a very bright fire, without allowing the bread to blacken, which spoils the appearance and flavour of all toast. When of a nice colour on both sides, put it on a hot plate; divide some good butter into small pieces, place them on the toast, set this before the fire and when the butter is just beginning to melt, spread it lightly over the toast. Trim off the crust and ragged edges, divide each round into four pieces and send the toast quickly to table. Some persons cut the slices of toast across from corner to corner, so making the pieces of a three-cornered shape. Soyer recommends that each slice should be cut into pieces as soon as it is buttered, and when all are ready, that they should be piled lightly on the dish they are intended to be served on. He says that by cutting through four or five slices at a time, all the butter is squeezed out of the upper ones, while the bottom one is swimming in fat liquid. It is highly essential to use good butter for making this dish.

Beyond Bread

Plain Buns

Ingredients

To every 2 lbs of flour allow 6 oz of moist sugar, ½ gill* of yeast, ½ pint of milk, ½ lb of butter, warm milk.

Mode

Put the flour into a basin, mix the sugar well with it, make a hole in the centre and stir in the yeast and milk (which should be lukewarm), with enough of the flour to make it the thickness of cream. Cover the basin over with a cloth and let the sponge rise in a warm place, which will be accomplished in about 1½ hours. Melt the butter but do not allow it to oil; stir it into the other ingredients, with enough warm milk to make the whole into a soft dough, then mould it into buns about the size of an egg; lay them in rows quite 3 inches apart; set them again in a warm place, until they have risen to double their size; then put them into a good brisk oven and just before they are done, wash them over with a little milk. From 15 to 20 minutes will be required to bake them nicely. These buns may be varied by adding a few currants, candied peel or caraway seeds to the other ingredients, and the above mixture answers for hot cross buns, by putting in a little ground allspice and by pressing a tin mould in the form of a cross in the centre of the bun.

Time

15 to 20 minutes.
Sufficient to make eighteen buns.
*[A gill is generally defined as 5 fluid ounces.]

To Make Good Plain Buns

Ingredients

1 lb of flour
6 oz of good butter
¼ lb of sugar
1 egg
Nearly ¼ pint of milk
2 small teaspoonfuls of baking powder
A few drops of essence of lemon

Mode

Warm the butter, without oiling it; beat it with a wooden spoon; stir the flour in gradually with the sugar and mix these ingredients well together. Make the milk lukewarm, beat up with it the yolk of the egg and the essence of lemon and stir these into the flour, etc. Add the baking powder, beat the dough well for about 10 minutes, divide it into twenty-four pieces, put them into buttered tins or cups and bake in a brisk oven from 20 to 30 minutes.

Time

20 to 30 minutes.
Sufficient to make twelve buns.

Light Buns

Ingredients

½ teaspoonfuls of tartaric acid
½ teaspoonfuls of bicarbonate of soda
1 lb of flour
2 oz of butter
2 oz of loaf sugar
¼ lb of currants or raisins, when liked
A few caraway seeds
½ pint of cold new milk
1 egg

Mode

Rub the tartaric acid, soda and flour all together through a hair sieve; work the butter into the flour; add the sugar, currants and caraway seeds, when the flavour of the latter is liked. Mix all these ingredients well together; make a hole in the middle of the flour and pour in the milk, mixed with the egg, which should be well beaten, mix quickly and set the dough, with a fork, on baking tins, and bake the buns for about 20 minutes. This mixture makes a very good cake and if put into a tin, should be baked for 1½ hours. The same quantity of flour, soda, and tartaric acid, with ½ pint of milk and a little salt, will make either bread or teacakes, if wanted quickly.

Time

20 minutes for the buns; if made into a cake, 1½ hours.
Sufficient to make about twelve buns.

Victoria Buns

Ingredients

2 oz of pounded loaf sugar
1 egg
1½ oz of ground rice
2 oz of butter

1½ oz of currants
A few thin slices of candied peel
Flour

Mode

Whisk the egg, stir in the sugar and beat these ingredients well together; beat the butter to a cream, stir in the ground rice, currants and candied peel, and as much flour as will make it of such a consistency that it may be rolled into seven or eight balls. Put these on to a buttered tin and bake them for ½ to ¾ hour. They should be put into the oven immediately or they will become heavy, and the oven should be tolerably brisk.

Time

½ to ¾ hour.
Sufficient to make seven or eight buns.

Crumpets

These are made in the same manner as muffins [see page 77]; only, in making the mixture, let it be more like batter than dough. Let it rise for about ½ hour; pour it into iron rings, which should be ready on a hotplate; bake them and when one side appears done, turn them quickly on to the other. To toast them, have ready a

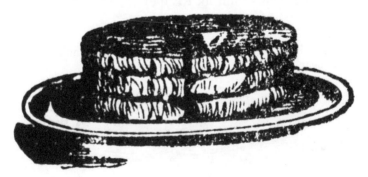

CRUMPETS.

very bright clear fire; put the crumpet on a toasting fork and hold it before the fire, *not too close*, until it is nicely brown on one side, but do not allow it to blacken. Turn it, and brown the other side, then spread it with good butter, cut it in half and, when all are done, pile them on a hot dish and send them quickly to table. Muffins and crumpets should always be served on separate dishes and both toasted and served as expeditiously as possible.

Time

From 10 to 15 minutes to bake them.

Sufficient

Allow two crumpets to each person.

Italian Rusks

A stale Savoy or lemon cake may be converted into very good rusks in the following manner. Cut the cake into slices, divide each slice in two; put them on a baking sheet, in a slow oven, and when they are of a nice brown and quite hard, they are done. They should be kept in a closed tin canister in a dry place, to preserve their crispness.

To Make Rusks (Suffolk Recipe)

Ingredients

To every lb of flour allow 2 oz of butter, ¼ pint of milk, 2 oz of loaf sugar, 3 eggs, 1 tablespoonful of yeast.

RUSKS.

Mode

Put the milk and butter into a saucepan and keep shaking it round until the latter is melted. Put the flour into a basin with the sugar, mix these well together and beat the eggs. Stir them with the yeast to the milk and butter, and with this liquid work the flour into a smooth dough. Cover a cloth over the basin and leave the dough to rise by the side of the fire, then knead it and divide it into twelve pieces; place them in a brisk oven and bake for about 20 minutes. Take the rusks out, break them in half and then then set them in the oven to get crisp on the other side. When cold, they should be put into tin canisters to keep them dry, and, if intended for the cheese course, the sifted sugar should be omitted.

Time

20 minutes to bake the rusks; 5 minutes to render them crisp after being divided.

Muffins

Ingredients

To every quart of milk allow 1½ oz of German yeast, a little salt, flour.

Mode

Warm the milk, add to it the yeast and mix these well together; put them into a pan and stir with sufficient flour to make the whole into a dough of rather a soft consistence; cover it over with a cloth and place it in a warm place to rise, and when light and nicely risen, divide the dough into pieces and round them to the proper shape with the hands; place them, in a layer of flour about two inches thick, on wooden trays, and let them rise again; when this is effected, each will exhibit a semi-globular shape. Then place them carefully on a hotplate or stove and bake them until they are slightly browned, turn them when they are done on one side. Muffins are not easily made and are more generally purchased than manufactured at home. To toast them,

MUFFINS.

divide the edge of the muffin all round, by pulling it open, to the depth of about an inch, with the fingers. Put it on a toasting fork and hold it before a very clear fire until one side is nicely browned but not burnt; turn and toast it on the other. Do not toast them too quickly, as, if this is done, the middle of the muffin will not be warmed through. When done, divide them by pulling them open; butter them slightly on both sides, put them together again and cut them into halves: when sufficient are toasted and buttered, pile them on a very hot dish and send them very quickly to table.

Time

From 20 minutes to ½ hour to bake them.

Sufficient

Allow one muffin to each person.

Tea Cakes

Ingredients

2 lbs of flour
½ teaspoonful of salt
¼ lb of butter or lard
1 egg
A piece of German yeast the size of a walnut
Warm milk

Mode

Put the flour (which should be perfectly dry) into a basin, mix with it the salt, and rub in the butter or lard; then beat the egg well, stir to it the yeast and add these to the flour with as much warm milk as will make the whole into a smooth paste, and knead it well. Let it rise near the fire and, when well risen, form it into cakes; place them on tins, let them rise again for a few minutes before putting them into the oven and bake from ¼ to ½ hour in a moderate oven. These are very nice with a few currants and a little sugar added to the other ingredients: they should be put in after the butter is rubbed in. These cakes should be buttered and eaten hot as soon as baked, but, when stale, they are very nice split and toasted, or if dipped in milk, or even water, and covered with a basin in the oven till hot, they will be almost equal to new.

Time

¼ to ½ hour.
Sufficient to make eight tea cakes.

To Toast Tea Cakes

Cut each tea cake into three or four slices, according to its thickness; toast them on both sides before a nice clear fire, and as each slice is done, spread it with butter on both sides. When a cake is toasted, pile the slices one on top of the other, cut them into quarters, put them on a very hot plate and send the cakes immediately to table. As they are wanted, send them in hot, one or two at a time, as, if allowed to stand, they spoil, unless kept in a muffin plate over a basin of boiling water.

Cakes

Almond Cake

Ingredients

9 oz of sweet almonds
6 eggs

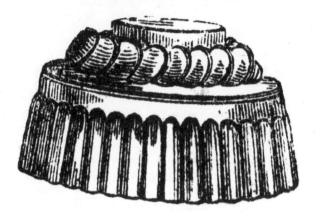

CAKE-MOULD.

8 tablespoonfuls of sifted sugar
5 tablespoonfuls of fine flour
The grated rind of 1 lemon
3 oz of butter

Mode

Blanch and pound the almonds to a paste; separate the whites from the yolks of the eggs; beat the latter and add them to the almonds. Stir in the sugar, flour and lemon rind; add the butter, which should be beaten to a cream; and when all these ingredients are well mixed, put in the whites of the eggs, which should be whisked to a stiff froth. Butter a cake mould, put in the mixture and bake in a good oven for 1¼ to 1¾ hours.

Time

1¼ hours to 1¾ hours.

Rich Bride or Christening Cake

Ingredients

5 lbs of the finest flour
3 lbs of fresh butter

BRIDE CAKE.

5 lbs of currants
2 lbs of sifted loaf sugar
2 nutmegs
¼ oz of mace
¼ oz of cloves
16 eggs
1 lb of sweet almonds
½ lb of candied citron
½ lb each of candied orange and lemon peel
1 gill* of wine
1 gill of brandy

Mode

Let the flour be as fine as possible and well dried and sifted; the currants washed, picked and dried before the fire; the sugar well pounded and sifted; the nutmegs grated, the spices pounded; the eggs thoroughly whisked, whites and yolks separately; the almonds pounded with a little orange flower water, and the candied peel cut in neat slices. When all these ingredients are prepared, mix them in the following manner. Begin working the butter with the hand till it becomes of a cream-like consistency; stir in the sugar and when the whites of the eggs are whisked to a solid froth, mix them with the butter and sugar. Next, well beat up the yolks for 10 minutes, and, adding them to the flour, nutmegs, mace and cloves, continue beating the whole together for ½ hour or longer, till wanted for the oven. Then mix in lightly the currants, almonds and candied peel with the wine and brandy, and having lined a hoop with buttered paper, fill it with the mixture and bake the cake in a tolerably quick oven, taking care, however, not to burn it: to prevent this, the top of it may be covered with a sheet of paper. To ascertain whether the cake is done, plunge a clean knife into the middle of it, withdraw it directly, and if the blade is not sticky and looks bright, the cake is sufficiently baked. These cakes are usually spread with a layer of almond icing, and over that another layer of sugar icing and afterwards ornamented. In baking a large cake like this, great attention must be paid to the heat of the oven; it should not be too fierce but have a good soaking heat.

Time

5 to 6 hours.
*[A gill is generally defined as 5 fluid ounces.]

Nice Breakfast Cakes

Ingredients

1 lb of flour
½ teaspoonful of tartaric acid
½ teaspoonful of salt
½ teaspoonful of carbonate of soda
1½ breakfast cupfuls of milk
1 oz of sifted loaf sugar
2 eggs

Mode

These cakes are made in the same manner as the soda bread, with the addition of eggs and sugar. Mix the flour, tartaric acid and salt well together, taking care that the two latter ingredients are reduced to the finest powder, and stir in the sifted sugar, which should also be very fine. Dissolve the soda in the milk, add the eggs, which should be well whisked, and with this liquid work the flour, etc., into a light dough. Divide it into small cakes, put them into the oven immediately and bake for about 20 minutes.

Time

20 minutes.

Common Cake, Suitable for Sending to Children at School

Ingredients

2 lbs of flour
4 oz of butter or clarified dripping
½ oz of caraway seeds
¼ oz of allspice
½ lb of pounded sugar
1 lb of currants
1 pint of milk
3 tablespoonfuls of fresh yeast

Mode

Rub the butter lightly into the flour, add all the dry ingredients, and mix these well together. Make the milk warm, but not hot; stir in the yeast, and with this liquid make the whole into a light dough; knead it well and line the cake tins with strips of buttered paper: this paper should be about 6 inches higher than the top of the tin. Put in the dough, stand it in a warm place to rise for more than an hour; then bake the cakes in a well-heated oven. If this quantity be divided in two, they will take from 1½ to 2 hours' baking.

Time

1¾ to 2¼ hours.
Sufficient to make two moderate-sized cakes.

Economical Cake

Ingredients

1 lb of flour
¼ lb of sugar
¼ lb of butter or lard
½ lb of currants
1 teaspoonful of carbonate of soda
The whites of 4 eggs
½ pint of milk

Mode

In making many sweet dishes, the whites of eggs are not required, and if well beaten and added to the above ingredients, make an excellent cake, with or without currants. Beat the butter to a cream, well whisk the whites of the eggs, and stir all the ingredients together but the soda, which must not be added until all is well mixed, and the cake is ready to be put into the oven. When the mixture has been well beaten, stir in the soda, put the cake into a buttered mould and bake it in a moderate oven for 1½ hours.

Time

1½ hours.

A Nice Useful Cake

Ingredients

¼ lb of butter
6 oz of currants
¼ lb of sugar
1 lb of dried flour
2 teaspoonfuls of baking powder

3 eggs
1 teacupful of milk
2 oz of sweet almonds
1 oz of candied peel

Mode

Beat the butter to a cream; wash, pick and dry the currants; whisk the eggs; blanch and chop the almonds and cut the peel into neat slices. When all these are ready, mix the dry ingredients together, then add the butter, milk and eggs and beat the mixture well for a few minutes.

Honey Cake

Ingredients

½ breakfast cupful of sugar
1 breakfast cupful of rich sour cream
2 breakfast cupfuls of flour
½ teaspoonful of carbonate of soda
Honey to taste

Mode

Mix the sugar and cream together; dredge in the flour with as much honey as will flavour the mixture nicely; stir it well, that all the ingredients may be thoroughly mixed; add the carbonate of soda, and beat the cake well for another five minutes; put it into a buttered tin, bake it from ½ to ¾ hour, and let it be eaten warm.

Time

½ to ¾ hour.
Sufficient for three or four persons.

Luncheon Cake

Ingredients

½ lb of butter
1 lb of flour

½ oz of caraway seeds
¼ lb of currants
6 oz of moist sugar
1 oz of candied peel
3 eggs
½ pint of milk
1 small teaspoonful of carbonate of soda

Mode

Rub the butter into the flour until it is quite fine; add the caraway seeds, currants (which should be nicely washed, picked and dried), sugar and candied peel cut into thin slices; mix these well together, and moisten with the eggs, which should be well whisked. Boil the milk and add to it, whilst boiling, the carbonate of soda, which must be well stirred into it, and, with the milk, mix the other ingredients. Butter a tin, pour the cake into it, and bake it in a moderate oven from ¾ to 1 hour.

Time

1 to 1½ hours.

A Pavini Cake

Ingredients

½ lb of flour
½ lb of ground rice
½ lb of raisins, stoned and cut into small pieces
¼ lb of currants
¼ lb of butter
2 oz of sweet almonds
¼ lb of sifted loaf sugar
½ nutmeg grated
1 pint of milk
1 teaspoonful of carbonate of soda

Mode

Stone and cut the raisins into small pieces; wash, pick and dry the currants; melt the butter to a cream, but without oiling it; blanch and chop the almonds and grate the nutmeg. When all these ingredients are thus prepared, mix them well together; make the milk warm, stir in the soda and with this liquid make the whole into a paste. Butter a mould, rather more than half fill it with the dough and bake the cake in a moderate oven from 1½ to 2 hours, or less time should it be made into 2 cakes.

Time

1½ to 2 hours.

A Nice Plain Cake

Ingredients

1 lb of flour
1½ teaspoonfuls of Borwick's baking powder
¼ lb of good dripping
1 teacupful of moist sugar
3 eggs
1 breakfast cupful of milk
1 oz of caraway seeds
¼ lb of currants

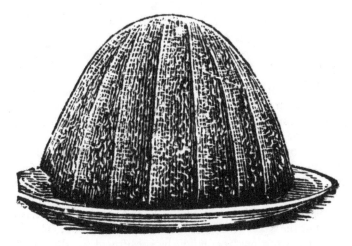

PLAIN CAKE.

Mode

Put the flour and baking powder into a basin; stir these together, then rub in the dripping, add the sugar, caraway seeds and currants, whisk the eggs with the milk and beat all together very thoroughly until the ingredients are well mixed. Butter a tin, put in the cake, and bake it from 1½ to 2 hours. Let the dripping be quite clean before using: to insure this, it is a good plan to clarify it. Beef dripping is better than any other for cakes, etc., as mutton dripping frequently has a very unpleasant flavour, which would be imparted to the preparation.

Time

1½ to 2 hours.

A Nice Plain Cake For Children

Ingredients

1 quartern of dough*
¼ lb of moist sugar
¼ lb of butter or good beef dripping
¼ pint of warm milk
½ grated nutmeg or ½ oz of caraway seeds

Mode

If you are not in the habit of making bread at home, procure the dough from the baker's, and, as soon as it comes in, put it into a basin near the fire; cover the basin with a thick cloth and let the dough remain a little while to rise. In the meantime, beat the butter to a cream and make the milk warm; and when the dough has risen, mix with it thoroughly all the above ingredients and knead the cake well for a few minutes. Butter some cake tins, half fill them, and stand them in a warm place, to allow the dough to rise again. When the tins are three-parts full, put the cakes into a good oven and bake them from 1¾ to 2 hours. A few currants might be substituted for the caraway seeds when the flavour of the latter is disliked.

Time

1¾ to 2 hours.
*[A quartern is generally defined as ¼ pint.]

Common Plum Cake

Ingredients

3 lbs of flour
6 oz of butter or good dripping
6 oz of moist sugar
6 oz of currants
½ oz of pounded allspice
2 tablespoonfuls of fresh yeast
1 pint of new milk

Mode

Rub the butter into the flour; add the sugar, currants and allspice; warm the milk, stir to it the yeast and mix the whole into a dough; knead it well and put it into six buttered tins; place them near the fire for nearly an hour for the dough to rise, then bake the cakes in a good oven from 1 to 1¼ hours. To ascertain when they are done, plunge a clean knife into the middle, and if on withdrawal it comes out clean, the cakes are done.

PLUM CAKE WITH ALMONDS.

Time

1 to 1¼ hours.
Sufficient to make six small cakes.

A Nice Plum Cake

Ingredients

1 lb of flour
¼ lb of butter
½ lb of sugar
½ lb of currants
2 oz of candied lemon peel
½ pint of milk
1 teaspoonful of carbonate of soda

Mode

Put the flour into a basin with the sugar, currants and sliced candied peel; beat the butter to a cream and mix all these ingredients together with the milk. Stir the soda into 2 tablespoonful of milk; add it to the dough and beat the whole well, until everything is thoroughly mixed. Put the dough into a buttered tin and bake the cake for 1½ to 2 hours.

Time

1½ to 2 hours.

Pound Cake

Ingredients

1 lb of butter
1¼ lbs of flour
1 lb of pounded loaf sugar
1 lb of currants
9 eggs
2 oz of candied peel
½ oz of citron

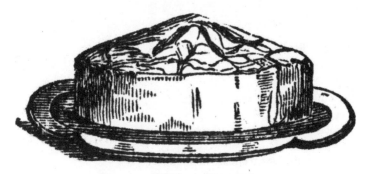

POUND CAKE.

½ oz of sweet almonds
When liked, a little pounded mace

Mode

Work the butter to a cream; dredge in the flour; add the sugar, currants, candied peel, which should be cut into neat slices, and the almonds, which should be blanched and chopped, and mix all these well together; whisk the eggs and let them be thoroughly blended with the dry ingredients. Beat the cake well for 20 minutes and put it into a round tin, lined at the bottom and sides with a strip of buttered paper. Bake it from 1½ to 2 hours, and let the oven be well heated when the cake is first put in, as, if this is not the case, the currants will all sink to the bottom of it. To make this preparation light, the yolks and whites of the eggs should be beaten separately, and added separately to the other ingredients. A glass of wine is sometimes added to the mixture; but this is scarcely necessary, as the cake will be found quite rich enough without it.

Time

1½ to 2 hours.

Sufficient

The above quantity divided in two will make two nice-sized cakes.

Queen Cakes

Ingredients

1 lb of flour
½ lb of butter
½ lb of pounded loaf sugar
3 eggs
1 teacupful of cream
½ lb of currants
1 teaspoonful of carbonate of soda
Essence of lemon or almonds to taste

Mode

Work the butter to a cream, dredge in the flour, add the sugar and currants and mix the ingredients well together. Whisk the eggs, mix them with the cream and flavouring and stir these to the flour; add the carbonate of soda, beat the paste well for 10 minutes, put it into small buttered pans, and bake the cakes from ¼ to ½ hour. Grated lemon rind may be substituted for the lemon and almond flavouring, which will make the cakes equally nice.

Time

¼ to ½ hour.

Rice Cake

Ingredients

½ lb of ground rice
½ lb of flour
½ lb of loaf sugar
9 eggs
20 drops of essence of lemon or the rind of 1 lemon
¼ of butter

Mode

Separate the whites from the yolks of the eggs; whisk them both well and add to the latter the butter, beaten to a cream. Stir in the flour, rice, and lemon (if the rind is used, it must be very finely minced) and beat the mixture well, then add the whites of the eggs, beat the cake again for some time, put it into a buttered mould or tin, and bake it for nearly 1½ hours. It may be flavoured with essence of almonds, when this is preferred.

Time

Nearly 1½ hours.

Saucer Cake for Tea

Ingredients

¼ lb of flour
¼ lb of *tous-les-mois**
¼ lb of pounded white sugar
¼ lb of butter
2 eggs
1 oz of candied orange or lemon peel

Mode

Mix the flour and *tous-les-mois* together; add the sugar, the candied peel cut into thin slices, the butter beaten to a cream and the eggs well whisked. Beat the mixture for 10 minutes, put it into a buttered cake tin or mould or, if this is not obtainable, a soup plate answers the purpose, lined with a piece of buttered paper. Bake the cake in a moderate oven from 1 to 1¼ hours, and when cold, put it away in a covered canister. It will remain good for some weeks, even if it be cut into slices.

Time

1 to 1¼ hours.
*[This is similar to arrowroot.]

Savoy Cake

Ingredients

7 eggs
The weight of 4 eggs in pounded loaf sugar

The weight of 7 in flour
A little grated lemon rind, or essence of almonds, or orange flower

Mode

Break the seven eggs, putting the yolks into one basin and the whites into another. Whisk the former, and mix with them the sugar, the grated lemon rind or any other flavouring to taste; beat them well together and add the whites of the eggs, whisked to a froth. Put in the flour by degrees, continuing to beat the mixture for ¼ hour, butter a mould, pour in the cake and bake it from 1¼ to 1½ hours. This is a very nice cake for dessert and may be iced for a supper table or cut into slices and spread with jam, which converts it into sandwiches.

Time

1¼ to 1½ hours.
Sufficient for one cake.

Scrap Cakes

Ingredients

2 lbs of leaf* or the inside fat of a pig
1½ lbs of flour
¼ lb of moist sugar
½ lb of currants
1 oz of candied lemon peel
Ground allspice to taste

Mode

Cut the leaf, or flead, as it is sometimes called, into small pieces; put it into a large dish, which place in a quick oven; be careful that it does not burn, and in a short time it will be reduced to oil, with the small pieces of leaf floating on the surface, and it is of these that the cakes should be made. Gather all the scraps together, put them into a basin with the flour, and rub them well together. Add the currants, sugar, candied peel, cut into thin slices, and the ground allspice. When all these ingredients are well mixed, moisten with sufficient cold water to make the whole into a nice paste; roll it out thin, cut it into shapes, and bake the cakes in a quick oven from 15 to 20 minutes. These are very economical and wholesome cakes for children, and the lard, melted at home, produced from the flead, is generally better than that you purchase. To prevent the lard from burning, and to insure its being a good colour, it is better to melt it in a jar placed in a saucepan of boiling water; by doing it in this manner, there will be no chance of its discolouring.

Time

15 to 20 minutes.
Sufficient to make three or four dozen cakes.
*[Leaf, or flead, is a type of fat from which lard was made.]

Common Seed Cake

Ingredients

½ quartern of dough*
¼ lb of good dripping
6 oz of moist sugar
½ oz of caraway seeds
1 egg

SEED CAKE.

Mode

If the dough is sent in from the baker's, put it in a basin covered with a cloth and set it in a warm place to rise. Then, with a wooden spoon, beat the dripping to a liquid; add it, with the other ingredients, to the dough and beat it until everything is very thoroughly mixed. Put it into a buttered tin and bake the cake for rather more than 2 hours.

Time

Rather more than 2 hours.
*[A quartern is generally defined as ¼ pint.]

A Very Good Seed Cake

Ingredients

1 lb of butter
6 eggs
¾ lb of sifted sugar
Pounded mace and grated nutmeg to taste
1 lb of flour
¾ oz caraway seeds
1 wineglassful of brandy

Mode

Beat the butter to a cream; dredge in the flour; add the sugar, mace, nutmeg, and caraway seeds and mix these ingredients well together. Whisk the eggs, stir to them the brandy, and beat the cake again for 20 minutes. Put it into a tin lined with buttered paper and bake it from 1½ to 2 hours. This cake would be equally nice made with currants and omitting the caraway seeds.

Time

1½ to 2 hours.

Snow Cake

Ingredients

½ lb of *tous-les-mois**
¼ lb of white pounded sugar

¼ lb of fresh or washed salt butter
1 egg
The juice of 1 lemon

Mode

Beat the butter to a cream, then add the egg, previously well beaten, and then the other ingredients; if the mixture is not light, add another egg and beat for ¼ hour, until it turns white and light. Line a flat tin, with raised edges, with a sheet of buttered paper; pour in the cake and put it into the oven. It must be rather slow, and the cake not allowed to brown at all. If the oven is properly heated, 1 to 1¼ hours will be found long enough to bake it. Let it cool a few minutes, then with a clean sharp knife cut it into small pieces, which should be gently removed to a large flat dish to cool before putting it away. This will keep for several weeks.

Time

1 to 1¼ hours.
*[This is similar to arrowroot.]

Snow Cake (A genuine Scotch Recipe)

Ingredients

1lb of arrowroot
½ lb of pounded white sugar
½ lb of butter
The whites of 6 eggs
Flavouring to taste, of essence to almonds, or vanilla, or lemon

Mode

Beat the butter to a cream; stir in the sugar and arrowroot gradually, at the same time beating the mixture. Whisk the whites of the eggs to a stiff froth, add them to the other ingredients and beat well for 20 minutes. Put in whichever of the above flavourings may be preferred; pour the cake into a buttered mould or tin and bake it in a moderate oven from 1 to 1½ hours.

Time

1 to 1½ hours.
Sufficient to make a moderate-sized cake.

Soda Cake

Ingredients

¼ lb of butter
1 lb of flour
½ lb of currants
½ lb of moist sugar
1 teacupful of milk
3 eggs
1 teaspoonful of carbonate of soda

Mode

Rub the butter into the flour, add the currants and sugar and mix these ingredients well together. Whisk the eggs well, stir them into the flour, etc., with the milk, in which the soda should be previously dissolved, and beat the whole up together with a wooden spoon or beater. Divide the dough into two pieces, put them into buttered moulds or cake tins and bake in a moderate oven for nearly an hour. The mixture must be extremely well beaten up and not allowed to stand after the soda is added to it, but must be placed in the oven immediately. Great care must also be taken that the cakes are quite done through, which may be ascertained by thrusting a knife into the middle of them: if the blade looks bright when withdrawn, they are done. If the tops acquire too much colour before the inside is sufficiently baked, cover them with a piece of clean paper to prevent them from burning.

Time

1 hour.
Sufficient to make two small cakes.

Sponge Cake I

Ingredients

8 eggs
The weight of 8 eggs in pounded loaf sugar
The weight of 5 in flour
The rind of 1 lemon
1 tablespoonful of brandy

Mode

Put the eggs into one side of the scale, and take the weight of 8 in pounded loaf sugar and the weight of 5 in good *dry* flour. Separate the yolks from the whites of the eggs; beat the former, put them into a saucepan with the sugar and let them remain over the fire until *milk-warm*, keeping them well stirred. Then put them into a basin, add the grated lemon rind mixed with the brandy, and stir these well together, dredging in the flour very gradually. Whisk the whites of the eggs to a very stiff froth, stir them to the flour, etc., and beat the cake well for ¼ hour. Put it

SPONGE CAKE.

into a buttered mould strewn with a little fine sifted sugar and bake the cake in a quick oven for 1½ hours. Care must be taken that it is put into the oven immediately or it will not be light. The flavouring of this cake may be varied by adding a few drops of essence of almonds instead of the grated lemon rind.

Time

1½ hours.
Sufficient for one cake.

Sponge Cake II

Ingredients

½ lb of loaf sugar
Not quite ¼ pint of water
5 eggs
1 lemon
½ lb of flour
¼ teaspoonful of carbonate of soda

Mode

Boil the sugar and water together until they form a thick syrup; let it cool a little, then pour it to the eggs, which should be previously well whisked; and after the eggs and syrup are mixed together, continue beating them for a few minutes. Grate the lemon rind, mix the carbonate of soda with the flour and stir these lightly to the other ingredients; then add the lemon juice, and when the whole is thoroughly mixed, pour it into a buttered mould and bake in rather a quick oven for rather more than 1 hour. The remains of sponge or Savoy cakes answer very well for trifles, light puddings, etc., and a very stale one (if not mouldy) makes an excellent tipsy cake.

Time

Rather more than 1 hour.
Sufficient to make one cake.

To Make Small Sponge Cakes

Ingredients

8 eggs
The weight of 5 eggs in flour
The weight of 8 in pounded loaf sugar
Flavouring to taste

Mode

Let the flour be perfectly dry, and the sugar well pounded and sifted. Separate the whites from the yolks of the eggs and beat the latter up with the sugar, then whisk the whites until they become rather stiff and mix them with the yolks, but do not stir them more than is just necessary to mingle the ingredients well together. Dredge in the flour by degrees, add the flavouring; butter the tins well, pour in the batter, sift a little sugar over the cakes and bake them in rather a quick oven, but do not allow them to take too much colour, as they should be rather pale. Remove them from the tins before they get cold and turn them on their faces, where let them remain until quite cold, when store them away in a closed tin canister or wide-mouthed glass bottle.

Time

10 to 15 minutes in a quick oven.

Victoria Sandwiches

Ingredients

4 eggs
Their weight in pounded sugar, butter and flour
½ saltspoonful of salt
A layer of any kind of jam or marmalade

Mode

Beat the butter to a cream; dredge in the flour and pounded sugar; stir these ingredients well together, and add the eggs, which should be previously thoroughly whisked. When the mixture has been well beaten for about 10 minutes, butter a Yorkshire pudding tin, pour in the batter and bake it in a moderate oven for 20 minutes. Let it cool, spread one half of the cake with a layer of nice preserve, place over it the other half of the cake, press the pieces slightly together and then cut it into long finger pieces; pile them in crossbars on a glass dish and serve.

Time

20 minutes.
Sufficient for five or six persons.

A Nice Yeast Cake

Ingredients

1½ lbs of flour
½ lb of butter
½ pint of milk
1½ tablespoonfuls of good yeast
3 eggs
¾ lb of currants
½ lb of white moist sugar
2 oz of candied peel

Mode

Put the milk and butter into a saucepan and shake it round over a fire until the butter is melted, but do not allow the milk to get very hot. Put the flour into a basin, stir to it the milk and butter, the yeast, and eggs, which should be well beaten, and form the whole into a smooth dough. Let it stand in a warm place, covered with a cloth, to rise, and, when sufficiently risen, add the currants, sugar, and candied peel cut into thin slices. When all the ingredients are thoroughly mixed, line two moderate-sized cake tins with buttered paper, which should be about 6 inches higher than the tin; pour in the mixture, let it stand to rise again for another ½ hour and then bake the cakes in a brisk oven for about 1½ hours. If the tops of them become too brown, cover them with paper until they are done through. A few drops of essence of lemon, or a little grated nutmeg, may be added when the flavour is liked.

Time

From 1¼ to 1½ hours.
Sufficient to make two moderate-sized cakes.

Icing for Cakes

Almond Icing For Cakes

Ingredients

To every lb of finely pounded loaf sugar allow 1 lb of sweet almonds, the whites of 4 eggs and a little rosewater.

Mode

Blanch the almonds and pound them (a few at a time) in a mortar to a paste, adding a little rosewater to facilitate the operation, whisk the whites of the eggs to a strong froth; mix them with the pounded almonds, stir in the sugar, and beat altogether. When the cake is sufficiently baked, lay on the almond icing and put it into the oven to dry. Before laying this preparation on the cake, great care must be taken that it is nice and smooth, which is easily accomplished by well beating the mixture.

Sugar Icing For Cakes

Ingredients

To every lb of loaf sugar allow the whites of 4 eggs, 1 oz of fine starch.

Mode

Beat the eggs to a strong froth and gradually sift in the sugar, which should be reduced to the finest possible powder, and gradually add the starch, also finely powdered. Beat the mixture well until the sugar is smooth, then with a spoon or a broad knife lay the icing equally over the cakes. These should then be placed in a very cool oven and the icing allowed to dry and harden but not to colour. The icing may be coloured with strawberry or currant juice. If it be put on the cakes as soon as they are withdrawn from the oven, it will become firm and hard by the time the cakes are cold. On very rich cakes, such as wedding, christening cakes, etc., a layer of almond icing, above, is usually spread over the top and over that the white icing as described. All iced cakes should be kept in a very dry place.

Pastry and Pies

Butter Crust, for Boiled Puddings

Ingredients

To every lb of flour allow 6 oz of butter, ½ pint of water.

Mode

With a knife, work the flour to a smooth paste with ½ pint of water; roll the crust out rather thin; place the butter over it in small pieces; dredge lightly over it some flour, and fold the paste over; repeat the rolling one more, and the crust will be ready for use. It may be enriched by adding another 2 oz of butter; but, for ordinary purposes, the above quantity will be found quite sufficient.

Common Paste for Family Use

Ingredients

1¼ lbs of flour
½ lb of butter
Rather more than ½ pint of water

Mode

Rub the butter lightly into the flour and mix it to a smooth paste with the water; roll it out two or three times, and it will be ready for use. This paste may be converted into an excellent short crust for sweet tarts, by adding to the flour, after the butter is rubbed in, 2 tablespoonfuls of finely sifted sugar.

Common Crust for Raised Pies

Ingredients

To every lb of flour allow ½ pint of water, 1½ oz of butter, 1½ oz of lard, ½ saltspoonful of salt.

Mode

Put into a saucepan the water; when it boils, add the butter and lard, and when these are melted, make a hole in the middle of the flour; pour in the water gradually; beat it well with a wooden spoon and be particular in not making the paste too soft. When it is well mixed, knead it with the hands until quite stiff, dredging a little flour over the paste and board to prevent them from sticking. When it is well kneaded, place it before the fire, with a cloth covered over it, for a few minutes; it will then be more easily worked into shape. This paste does not taste so nicely as the preceding one, but is worked with greater facility, and answers just as well for raised pies, for the crust is seldom eaten.

Dripping Crust, for Kitchen Puddings, Pies, etc.

Ingredients

To every lb of flour allow 6 oz of clarified beef dripping, ½ pint of water.

Mode

After having clarified the dripping, weigh it and to every lb of flour allow the above proportion of dripping. With a knife, work the flour into a smooth paste with the water, rolling it out three times, each time placing on the crust 2 oz of the dripping, broken into small pieces. If this paste is lightly made, if good dripping is used, and *not too much* of it, it will be found good; and by the addition of 2 tablespoonfuls of fine moist sugar, it may be converted into a common short crust for fruit pies.

Lard or Flead Crust

Ingredients

To every lb of flour allow ½ lb of lard or flead*, ½ pint of water, ½ saltspoonful of salt.

Mode

Clear the flead free of skin and slice it into thin flakes; rub it into the flour, add the salt and work the whole into a smooth paste, with the above proportion of water; fold the paste over two or three times, beat it well with the rolling pin, roll it out and it will be ready for use. The crust made from this will be found extremely light and may be made into cakes or tarts; it may also be very much enriched by adding more flead to the same proportion of flour.

*[Flead is a type of fat from which lard was made.]

Pate Brisée, or French Crust, for Raised Pies

Ingredients

To every lb of flour allow ½ saltspoonful of salt, 2 eggs, ⅓ pint of water, 6 oz of butter.

Mode

Spread the flour, which should be sifted and thoroughly dry, on the paste board; make a hole in the centre, into which put the butter; work it lightly into the flour and, when quite fine, add the salt; work the whole into a smooth paste with the eggs (yolks and whites) and water and make it very firm. Knead the paste well and let it be rather stiff, that the sides of the pie may be easily raised and that they do not afterwards tumble or shrink.

Note: This paste may be very much enriched by making it with equal quantities of flour and butter, but then it is not so easily raised as when made plainer.

French Puff Paste or Feuilletage
(founded on M. Ude's Recipe)

Ingredients

Equal quantities of flour and butter – say 1 lb of each
½ saltspoonful of salt
The yolks of 2 eggs
Rather more than ¼ pint of water

Mode

Weigh the flour; ascertain that it is perfectly dry, and sift it; squeeze all the water from the butter and wring it in a clean cloth till there is no moisture remaining. Put the flour on the paste board, work lightly into it 2 oz of the butter and then make a hole in the centre, into this well put the yolks of two eggs, the salt and about ¼ pint of water (the quantity of this latter ingredient must be regulated by the cook, as it is impossible to give the exact proportion of it); knead up the paste quickly and lightly, and, when quite smooth, roll it out square to the thickness of about ½ inch. Presuming that the butter is perfectly free from moisture, and as cool as possible, roll it into a ball, and place this ball of butter on the paste; fold the paste over the butter all round and secure by wrapping it well all over. Flatten the paste by rolling it lightly with the rolling pin until it is quite thin, but not thin enough to allow the butter to break through, and keep the board and paste dredged lightly with lightly with flour during the process of making it. This rolling gives it the *first* turn. Now fold the paste in three and roll out again, and, should the weather be very warm, put it in a cold place on the ground to cool between the several turns; for unless this is particularly attended to, the paste will be spoiled. Roll out the paste again twice, put it by to cool, then roll it out twice more, which will make six turnings in all. Now fold the paste in two and it will be ready for use. If properly baked and well made, this crust will be delicious and should rise in the oven about 5 or 6 inches. The paste should be made rather firm in the first instance, as the ball of butter is liable to break through. Great attention must be also be paid to keeping the butter very cool, as, if this is in a liquid and soft state, the paste will not answer at all. Should the cook be dexterous enough to succeed in making this, the paste will have a much better appearance than that made by the process of dividing the butter into four parts, and placing it over the rolled-out paste, but until experience has been acquired, we recommend puff paste. The above paste is used for vols-au-vent, small articles of pastry, and, in fact, everything that requires very light crust.

Medium Puff Paste

Ingredients

To every lb of flour allow 8 oz of butter, 4 oz of lard, not quite ½ pint of water.

Mode

This paste may be made by the directions in the preceding recipe, only using less butter and substituting lard for a portion of it. Mix the flour to a smooth paste with not quite ½ pint of water; then roll it out three times, the first time covering the paste with butter, the second with lard, and third with butter, and it will be ready for use. Keep the rolling pin and paste slightly dredged, to prevent them from sticking.

Soyer's Recipe for Puff Paste

Ingredients

To every lb of flour allow the yolk of 1 egg, the juice of 1 lemon, ½ saltspoonful of salt, cold water, 1 lb of fresh butter.

Mode

Put the flour on to the paste board; make a hole in the centre, into which put the yolk of the egg, the lemon juice and salt; mix the whole with cold water (this should be iced in summer, if convenient) into a soft flexible paste, with the right hand, and handle it as little as possible, then squeeze all the buttermilk from the butter, wring it in a cloth and roll out the paste; place the butter on this and fold the edges of the paste over, so as to hide it; roll it out again to the thickness of ¼ inch; fold over one third, over which again pass the rolling pin; then fold over the other third, thus forming a square; place it with the ends, top and bottom before you, shaking a little flour both under and over and repeat the rolls and turns twice again, as before. Flour a baking sheet, put the paste on this and let it remain on ice or in some cool place for ½ hour; then roll twice more, turning it as before; place it again upon the ice for ¼ hour, give it two more rolls, making seven in all, and it is ready for use when required.

Very Good Puff Paste

Ingredients

To every lb of flour allow 1 lb of butter and not quite ½ pint of water.

Mode

Carefully weigh the flour and butter, and have the exact proportion; squeeze the butter well to extract the water from it, and afterwards wring it in a clean cloth, that no moisture may remain. Sift the flour; see that it is perfectly dry and proceed in the following manner to make the paste, using a very *clean* paste board and rolling pin. Supposing the quantity to be 1 lb of flour, work the whole into a smooth paste, with not quite ½ pint of water, using a knife to mix it with; the proportion of this latter ingredient must be regulated by the discretion of the cook; if too much be added, the paste, when baked, will be tough. Roll it out until it is of an equal thickness of about an inch; break 4 oz of the butter into small pieces; place these on the paste, sift over it a little flour, fold it over, roll out again and put another 4 oz of butter. Repeat the rolling and buttering until the paste has been rolled out four times, or equal quantities of flour and butter have been used. Do not omit, every time the paste is rolled out, to dredge a little flour over that and the rolling pin, to prevent both from sticking. Handle the paste as lightly as possible and do not press heavily upon it with the rolling pin.

The next thing to be considered is the oven, as the baking of pastry requires particular attention. Do not put it into the oven until it is sufficiently hot to raise the paste, for the best prepared paste, if not properly baked, will be good for nothing. Brushing the paste as often as rolled out and the pieces of butter placed thereon, with the white of an egg, assists it to rise in leaves or flakes. As this is the great beauty of puff paste, it is well to try this method.

Recipes Using Puff Paste

Almond Flowers

Ingredients

Puff paste; to every ½ lb of paste allow 3 oz of almonds, sifted sugar, the white of an egg.

Mode

Roll the paste out to the thickness of ¼ inch and, with a round fluted cutter, stamp out as many pieces as may be required. Work the paste up again, roll it out and, with a smaller cutter, stamp out some pieces the size of a shilling. Brush the larger pieces over with the white of an egg, and place one of the smaller pieces on each. Blanch and cut the almonds into strips lengthwise; press them slanting into the paste closely round the rings; and when they are all completed, sift over some pounded sugar and bake for about ¼ hour or 20 minutes. Garnish between the almonds with strips of apple jelly and place in the centre of the ring a small quantity of strawberry jam; pile them high on the dish and serve.

Beef Rolls

Ingredients

The remains of cold roast or boiled beef
Seasoning to taste of salt, pepper and minced herbs
Puff paste

Mode

Mince the beef tolerably fine with a small amount of its own fat; add a seasoning of pepper, salt and chopped herbs; put the whole into a roll of puff paste and bake for ½ hour, or rather longer, should the roll be very large. Beef patties may be made of cold meat, by mincing and seasoning beef as directed above and baking in a rich puff paste in patty tins.

Time

½ hour.

Chicken or Fowl Patties

Ingredients

The remains of cold roast chicken or fowl
To every ¼ lb of meat allow 2 oz of ham, 3 tablespoonfuls of cream, 2 tablespoonfuls of veal gravy, ½ teaspoonful of minced lemon peel, cayenne, salt and pepper to taste, 1 tablespoonful of lemon juice, 1 oz of butter rolled in flour
Puff paste

Mode

Mince very small the white meat from a roast fowl, after removing all the skin; weigh it, and to every ¼ lb of meat allow the above proportion of minced ham. Put these into a stewpan with the remaining ingredients, stir over the fire for 10 minutes or ¼ hour, taking care that the mixture does not burn. Roll out some puff paste about ¼ inch in thickness; line the pattypans with this, put upon each a small piece of bread and cover with another layer of paste; brush over with the yolk of an egg, and bake in a brisk oven for ¼ hour. When done, cut a round piece out of the top and with a small spoon, take out the bread (be particular in not breaking the outside border of the crust) and fill the patties with the mixture.

Time

¼ hour to prepare the meat; not quite ¼ hour to bake the crust.

Chicken or Fowl Pie

Ingredients

2 small fowls or 1 large one
White pepper and salt to taste
½ teaspoonful of grated nutmeg
½ teaspoonful of pounded mace
Forcemeat*
A few slices of ham
3 hard-boiled eggs
½ pint of water
Puff crust

Mode

Skin and cut up the fowls into joints and put the neck, legs, and backbones in a stewpan, with a little water, an onion, a bunch of savoury herbs and a blade of mace; let these stew for about an hour and, when done, strain off the liquor: this is for gravy. Put a layer of fowl at the bottom of a pie dish, then a layer of ham, then one of forcemeat and hard-boiled eggs cut in rings; between the layers put a seasoning of pounded mace, nutmeg, pepper and salt. Proceed in this manner until the dish is full, and pour in about ½ pint of water; border the edge of the dish with puff crust, put on the cover, ornament the top and glaze it by brushing over it the yolk of an egg. Bake from 1¼ to 1½ hours, should the pie be very large, and, when done, pour in, at the top, the gravy made from the bones. If to be eaten cold, and wished particularly nice, the joints of the fowls should be boned and placed in the dish with alternate layers of forcemeat; sausage meat may also be substituted for the forcemeat and is now very much used. When the chickens are boned and mixed with sausage meat, the pie will take about 2 hours to bake. It should be covered with a piece of paper when about half done, to prevent the paste from being dried up or scorched.

Time

For a pie with unboned meat, 1¼ to 1½ hours; with boned meat and sausage or forcemeat, 1½ to 2 hours.
Sufficient for eight persons.

*[Forcemeat for a pie like this would consist of chopped bacon, suet, lemon rind, herbs, cayenne, mace and breadcrumbs, bound with eggs.]

Darioles a la Vanille (Sweet Entremets)

Ingredients

½ pint of milk
½ pint of cream
2oz of flour
3 oz of pounded sugar
6 eggs
2 oz of butter
Puff paste
Flavouring of essence of vanilla

Mode

Mix the flour to a smooth batter with the milk; stir in the cream, sugar, the eggs, which should be well whisked, and the butter, which should be beaten to a cream. Put in some essence of vanilla, drop by drop, until the mixture is well flavoured; line some dariole moulds with puff paste, three-parts fill them with the batter and bake in a good oven from 25 to 35 minutes. Turn them out of the moulds on a dish, without breaking them; strew over sifted sugar and serve. The flavouring of the darioles may be varied by substituting lemon, cinnamon or almonds, for the vanilla.

Time

25 to 35 minutes.
Sufficient to fill six or seven dariole moulds.

Fanchonnettes, or Custard Tartlets

Ingredients

For the custard:
4 eggs
¾ pint of milk
2 oz of butter

2 oz of pounded sugar
3 dessertspoonfuls of flour
Flavouring to taste

For the icing:
The whites of 2 eggs
2 oz of pounded sugar

Mode

Well beat the eggs; stir to them the milk, the butter, which should be beaten to a cream, the sugar, and flour; mix these ingredients well together, put them into a very clean saucepan and bring them to the simmering point, but do not allow them to boil. Flavour with essence of vanilla, lemon, grated chocolate or any flavouring ingredient that may be preferred. Line some round tartlet pans with good puff paste; fill them with the custard and bake in a moderate oven for about 20 minutes, then take them out of the pans; let them cool, and in the meantime, whisk the whites of the eggs to a stiff froth; stir into this the pounded sugar and spread smoothly over the tartlets a little of this mixture. Put them in the oven again to set the icing, but be particular that they do not scorch: when the icing looks crisp, they are done. Arrange them, piled high in the centre, on a white napkin, and garnish the dish, and in between the tartlets, with strips of bright jelly or very firmly made preserve.

Time

20 minutes to bake the tartlets; 5 minutes after being iced.
Sufficient to fill ten or twelve tartlets.

Note: The icing may be omitted on the top of the tartlets, and a spoonful of any kind of preserve put at the bottom of the custard instead: this varies both the flavour and appearance of this dish.

Fluted Rolls

Ingredients

Puff paste
The white of an egg

Sifted sugar
Jelly or preserve

Mode

Make some good puff paste by the recipe on page 107 (trimmings answer very well for little dishes of this sort); roll it out to the thickness of ¼ inch and, with a round fluted paste cutter, stamp out as many round pieces as may be required; brush over the upper side with the white of an egg; roll up the pieces, pressing the paste lightly together where it joins; place the rolls on a baking sheet, and bake for about ¼ hour. A few minutes before they are done, brush them over with the white of an egg; strew over sifted sugar, put them back into the oven; and when the icing is firm and of a pale brown colour, they are done. Place a strip of jelly or preserve across each roll, dish them high on a napkin and serve cold.

Time

¼ hour before being iced; 5 to 10 minutes after.
Sufficient: ½ lb of puff paste for two dishes.

Fruit Turnovers (Suitable for Picnics)

Ingredients

Puff paste (see recipe for medium puff paste on page 108)
Any kind of fruit
Sugar to taste

Mode

Make some puff paste; roll it out to the thickness of about ¼ inch and cut it out in pieces of a circular form; pile the fruit on half of the paste, sprinkle over some sugar, wet the edges and turn the paste over. Press the edges together, ornament them and brush the turnovers over with the white of an egg; sprinkle over sifted sugar and bake on tins, in a brisk oven, for about 20 minutes. Instead of putting the fruit in raw, it may be boiled down with a little sugar first and then inclosed in the crust; or jam of any kind, may be substituted for fresh fruit.

Time

20 minutes.
Sufficient: ½ lb of puff paste will make a dozen turnovers.

Lobster Patties (an Entrée)

Ingredient

Minced lobster
4 tablespoonfuls of béchamel
6 drops of anchovy sauce
Lemon juice
Cayenne to taste

Mode

Line the pattypans with puff paste and put into each a small piece of bread; cover with paste, brush over with egg, and bake of a light colour. Take as much lobster as is required, mince the meat very fine, and add the above ingredients; stir it over the fire for 5 minutes; remove the lids of the patty cases, take out the bread, fill with the mixture and replace the covers.

Time

About 5 minutes after the patty cases are made.

Mutton Pie (Puff Crust)

Ingredients

2 lbs of the neck or loin of mutton, weighed after being boned
2 kidneys
Pepper and salt
2 teacupfuls of gravy or water
2 tablespoonfuls of minced parsley
When liked, a little minced onion or shalot
Puff crust

Mode

Bone the mutton and cut the meat into steaks of all the same thickness and leave but very little fat. Cut up the kidneys and arrange these with the with the meat neatly in a pie dish; sprinkle over them the minced parsley and a seasoning of pepper and salt; pour in the gravy and cover with a tolerably good puff crust. Bake for 1½ hours, or rather longer, should the pie be very large, and let the oven be rather brisk. A well-made suet crust may be used instead of puff crust and will be found exceedingly good.

Time

1½ hours, or rather longer.
Sufficient for five or six persons.

Pastry Ramakins, to Serve With the Cheese Course

Ingredients

Any pieces of very good light puff paste
Cheshire, Parmesan or Stilton cheese

Mode

The remains or odd pieces of paste left from large tarts, etc. answer for making these little dishes. Gather up the pieces of paste, roll it out evenly and sprinkle it with grated cheese of a nice flavour. Fold the paste in three, roll it out again and sprinkle more cheese over; fold the paste, roll it out and with a paste cutter shape it in any way that may be desired. Bake the ramakins in a brisk oven from 10 to 15 minutes, dish them on a hot napkin, and serve quickly. The appearance of this dish may be very much improved by brushing the ramakins over with yolk of egg before they are placed in the oven. Where expense is not objected to, Parmesan is the best kind of cheese to use for making this dish.

Time

10 to 15 minutes.
Sufficient for six or seven persons.

Pastry Sandwiches

Ingredients

Puff paste
Jam of any kind
The white of an egg
Sifted sugar

Mode

Roll the paste out thin; put half of it on a baking sheet or tin, and spread equally over it apricot, greengage, or any preserve that may be preferred. Lay over this preserve another thin paste; press the edges together all round; and mark the paste in lines with a knife on the surface, to show where to cut it when baked. Bake from 20 minutes to ½ hour, and, a short time before being done, take the pastry out of the oven, brush it over with the white of an egg, sift over pounded sugar, and put it back in the oven to colour. When cold, cut it into strips; pile these on a dish pyramidically, and serve. These strips, cut about 2 inches long, piled in circular rows, and a plateful of flavoured whipped cream poured in the middle, make a very pretty dish.

Time

20 minutes to ½ hour.

Sufficient

½ lb of paste will make two dishes of sandwiches.

Pigeon Pie (Epsom Grand-Stand Recipe)

Ingredients

1½ lb of rump steak
2 or 3 pigeons
3 slices of ham
Pepper and salt to taste
2 oz of butter

4 eggs
Puff crust

Mode

Cut the steak into pieces about 3 inches square and with it line the bottom of a pie dish, seasoning it well with pepper and salt. Clean the pigeons, rub them with pepper and salt inside and out, and put in the body of each rather more than ½ oz of butter; lay them on the steak, and a piece of ham on each pigeon. Add the yolks of 4 eggs and half fill the dish with stock; place a border of puff paste round the edge of the dish, put on the cover and ornament it in any way that may be preferred. Clean three of the feet and place them in a hole made in the crust at the top: this shows what kind of pie it is. Glaze the crust, that is to say, brush it over with the yolk of an egg, and bake it in a well-heated oven for about 1¼ hours. When liked, a seasoning of pounded mace may be added.

Time

1¼ hours, or rather less.
Sufficient for five or six persons.

Polish Tartlets

Ingredients

Puff paste
The white of an egg
Pounded sugar

Mode

Roll some good puff paste out thin and cut it into 2½-inch squares; brush each square over with the white of an egg, then fold down the corners, so that they all meet in the middle of each piece of paste; slightly press the two pieces together, brush them over with the egg, sift over sugar and bake in a nice quick oven for about ¼ hour. When they are done, make a little hole in the middle of the paste and fill it up with apricot jam, marmalade or redcurrant jelly. Pile them high in the centre of a dish, on a napkin, and garnish with the same preserve the tartlets are filled with.

Time

¼ hour or 20 minutes.
Sufficient for two dishes of pastry.

Note: It should be borne in mind that for all dishes of small pastry, such as the preceding, trimmings of puff paste, left from larger tarts, answer as well as making the paste expressly.

Puits d'Amour, or Puff Paste Rings

Ingredients

French puff paste (see page 107)
The white of an egg
Sifted loaf sugar

Mode

Make some good puff paste by the recipe on page 107; roll it out to the thickness of about ¼ inch and, with a round fluted paste cutter, stamp out as many pieces as may be required; then work the paste up again and roll it out to the same thickness, and with a smaller cutter, stamp out sufficient pieces to correspond with the larger ones. Again stamp out the centre of these smaller rings; brush over the others with the white of an egg, place a small ring on the top of every large circular piece of paste, egg over the tops and bake from 15 to 20 minutes. Sift over sugar, put them back in the oven to colour them, then fill the rings with preserve of any bright colour. Dish them high on a napkin and serve. So many pretty dishes of pastry may be made by stamping puff paste out with fancy cutters and filling the pieces, when baked, with jelly or preserve, that our space will not allow us to give a separate recipe for each of them, but as they are all made from one paste, and only the shape and garnishing varied, perhaps it is not necessary, and, by exercising a little ingenuity, variety may always be obtained. Half-moons, leaves, diamonds, stars, shamrocks, rings, etc., are the most appropriate shapes for pastry.

Time

15 to 25 minutes.
Sufficient for two dishes of pastry.

Tartlets

Ingredients

Trimmings of puff paste
Any jam or marmalade that may be preferred

Mode

Roll out the paste to the thickness of about ½ inch; butter some small round pattypans, line them with it and cut off the superfluous paste close to the edge of the pan. Put a small piece of bread into each tartlet (this is to keep them in shape) and bake in a brisk oven for about 10 minutes, or rather longer. When they are done, and are of a nice colour, take the pieces of bread out carefully and replace them by a spoonful of jam or marmalade. Dish them high on a white d'oyley, piled high in the centre, and serve.

Time

10 to 15 minutes.

Sufficient

1 lb of paste will make two dishes of tartlets.

Vol-au-Vent (an Entrée)

Ingredients

¾ to 1 lb of French puff paste
Fricasséed chickens, rabbits, ragouts or the remains of cold fish, flaked and warmed in thick white sauce

Mode

Make from ¾ to 1 lb of puff paste by the recipe on page 107, taking care that it is very evenly rolled out each time to insure

VOL-AU-VENT.

its rising properly, and if the paste is not extremely light, and put into a good hot oven, this cannot be accomplished, and the vol-au-vent will look very badly. Roll out the paste to the thickness of about 1½ inches, and, with a fluted cutter, stamp it out to the desired shape, either round or oval and, with the point of a small knife, make a slight incision in the paste all round the top, about an inch from the edge, which, when baked, forms the lid. Put the vol-au-vent into a good brisk oven and keep the door shut for a few minutes after it is put in. Particular attention should be paid to the heating of the oven, for the paste cannot rise without a tolerable degree of heat. When of a nice colour, without being scorched, withdraw it from the oven, instantly remove the cover where it was marked, and detach all the soft crumb from the centre: in doing this, be careful not to break the edges of the vol-au-vent, but should they look thin in places, stop them with small flakes of the inside paste, stuck on with the white of an egg. This precaution is necessary to prevent the fricassée or ragoût from bursting the case and so spoiling the appearance of the dish. Fill the vol-au-vent with a rich mince, or fricassee, or ragoût, or the remains of cold fish flaked and warmed in a good white sauce, and do not make them very liquid, for fear of the gravy bursting the crust, replace the lid and serve. To improve the appearance of the crust, brush it over with the yolk of an egg after it has risen properly.

Time

¾ hour to bake the vol-au-vent.

Note: Small vol-au-vents may be made and filled with minced veal, chicken, etc. They should be made of the same paste as the larger ones and stamped out with a small fluted cutter.

Common Short Crust

Ingredients

To every lb of flour allow 2 oz of sifted sugar, 3 oz of butter, about ½ pint of boiling milk.

Mode

Crumble the butter into the flour as finely as possible, add the sugar, and work the whole up to a smooth paste with the boiling milk. Roll it out thin and bake in a moderate oven.

Another Good Short Crust

Ingredients

To every lb of flour of flour allow 8 oz of butter, the yolks of 2 eggs, 2 oz of sifted sugar, about ¼ pint of milk.

Mode

Rub the butter into the flour, add the sugar, and mix the whole as lightly as possible to a smooth paste, with the yolks of eggs well beaten, and the milk. The proportion of the latter ingredient must be judged of by the size of the eggs; if these are large, so much will not be required, and more if the eggs are smaller.

Very Good Short Crust for Fruit Tarts

Ingredients

To every lb of flour allow ¾ lb of butter, 1 tablespoonful of sifted sugar, ⅓ pint of water.

Mode

Rub the butter into the flour, after having ascertained that the latter is perfectly dry; add the sugar, and mix the whole into a stiff paste, with about ⅓ pint of water. Roll it out two or three times, folding the paste over each time, and it will be ready for use.

Recipes Using Plain or Short Crust

Beefsteak Pie

Ingredients

3 lbs of rump steak
Seasoning to taste, of salt, cayenne, and black pepper
Crust
Water
The yolk of an egg

Mode

Have the steaks cut from a rump that has hung a few days, that they may be tender, and be particular that every portion is perfectly sweet. Cut the steaks into pieces about 3 inches long and 2 wide, allowing a *small* piece of fat to each piece of lean and arrange the meat in layers in a pie dish. Between each layer sprinkle a seasoning of salt, pepper, and, when liked, a few grains of cayenne. Fill the dish sufficiently with meat to support

BEEF-STEAK PIE.

the crust, and to give it a nice raised appearance when baked, and not to look flat and hollow. Pour in sufficient water to half fill the dish and border it with paste; brush it over with a little water and put on the cover; slightly press down the edges with the thumb and trim off close to the dish. Ornament the pie with leaves or pieces of paste cut in any shape that fancy may direct, brush it over with the beaten yolk of an egg; make a hole in the top of the crust and bake in a hot oven for about 1½ hours.

Time

In a hot oven, 1½ hours.
Sufficient for six or eight persons.

Giblet Pie

Ingredients

A set of duck or goose giblets
1 lb of rump steak
1 onion
½ teaspoonful of whole black pepper
A bunch of savoury herbs
Plain crust

Mode

Clean and put the giblets into a stewpan with an onion, whole pepper and a bunch of savoury herbs; add rather more than a pint of water and simmer gently for about 1½ hours. Take them out, let them cool and cut them into pieces; line the bottom of a pie dish with a few pieces of rump steak; add a layer of giblets and a few more pieces of steak; season with pepper and salt, and pour in the gravy (which should be strained), that the giblets were stewed in; cover with a plain crust, and bake for rather more than 1½ hours in a brisk oven. Cover a piece of paper over the pie, to prevent the crust taking too much colour.

Time

1½ hours to stew the giblets; about 1 hour to bake the pie.
Sufficient for five or six persons.

Mutton Pie (Any Crust)

Ingredients

The remains of a cold leg, loin or neck of mutton
Pepper and salt to taste
2 blades of pounded mace
1 dessertspoonful of chopped parsley
1 teaspoonful of minced savoury herbs
When liked, a little minced onion or shalot
3 or 4 potatoes
1 teacupful of gravy
Crust

Mode

Cold mutton may be made into very good pies if well seasoned and mixed with a few herbs; if the leg is used, cut it into very thin slices; if the loin or neck, into thin cutlets. Place some at the bottom of the dish; season well with pepper, salt, mace, parsley and herbs, then put a layer of potatoes sliced, then more mutton and so on till the dish is full; add the gravy, cover with a crust and bake for 1 hour.

Time

1 hour.

Suet Crust, for Pies or Puddings

Ingredients

To every lb of flour allow 5 or 6 oz of beef suet, ½ pint of water.

Mode

Free the suet from skin and shreds; chop it extremely fine and rub it well into the flour; work the whole to a smooth paste with the above proportion of water; roll it out and it is ready for use. This crust is quite rich enough for ordinary purposes, but when a better one is desired, use from ½ to ¾ lb of suet to every lb of flour. Some cooks, for rich crusts, pound the suet in a mortar, with a small quantity of butter. It should then be laid on the paste in small pieces, the same as for puff crust, and will be found exceedingly nice for hot tarts. 5 oz of suet to every lb of flour will make a very good crust and even ¼ lb will answer very well for children, or where the crust is wanted very plain.

To Ice or Glaze Pastry

To glaze pastry, which is the usual method adopted for meat or raised pies, break an egg, separate the yolk from the white, and beat the former for a short time. Then, when the pastry is nearly baked, take it out of the oven, brush it over with this beaten yolk of egg, and put it back in the oven to set the glaze.

To ice pastry, which is the usual method adopted for fruit tarts and sweet dishes of pastry, put the white of an egg on a plate, and with the blade of a knife beat it to a stiff froth. When the pastry is nearly baked, brush it over with this and sift over some pounded sugar; put it back into the oven to set the glaze, and, in a few minutes, it will be done. Great care should be taken that the paste does not catch or burn in the oven, which it is very liable to do after the icing is laid on.

Sufficient: Allow 1 egg and 1½ oz of sugar to glaze three tarts.

Puddings

Almond Cheesecakes

Ingredients

¼ lb of sweet almonds
3 eggs
2 oz of butter
The rind of ¼ lemon
1 tablespoonful of lemon juice
3 oz of sugar

Mode

Blanch and pound the almonds smoothly in a mortar, with a little rose or spring water; stir in the eggs, which should be well beaten, and the butter, which should be warmed; add the grated lemon peel and juice, sweeten and stir well until the whole is thoroughly mixed. Line some pattypans with puff paste, put in the mixture and bake for 20 minutes, or rather less, in a quick oven.

Time

20 minutes, or rather less.
Sufficient for about twelve cheesecakes.

Almond Paste, for Second-Course Dishes

Ingredients

1 lb of sweet almonds
1 lb of very finely sifted sugar
The whites of 2 eggs

Mode

Blanch the almonds and dry them thoroughly; put them into a mortar and pound them well, wetting them gradually with the whites of two eggs. When well pounded, put them into a small preserving pan, add the sugar and place the pan on a small but clear fire (a hotplate is better); keep stirring until the paste is dry, then take it out of the pan, put it between two dishes and, when cold, make it into any shape that fancy may dictate.

Time

½ hour.
Sufficient for three small dishes.

Baked Almond Pudding

Ingredients

¼ lb of almonds
1 glass of sherry

4 eggs
The rind and juice of ½ lemon
3 oz of butter
1 pint of cream
1 tablespoonful of sugar

Mode

Blanch and pound the almonds to a smooth paste with the water; mix these with the butter, which should be melted; beat up the eggs, grate the lemon rind and strain the juice; add these, with the cream, sugar and sherry, to the other ingredients and stir them well together. When well mixed, put it into a pie dish lined with puff paste and bake for ½ hour.

Time

½ hour.
Sufficient for four or five persons.

Note:
To make this pudding more economically, substitute milk for the cream, but then add rather more than 1 oz of finely grated bread.

Small Almond Puddings

Ingredients

½ lb of sweet almonds
¼ lb of butter
4 eggs
2 tablespoonfuls of sifted sugar
2 tablespoonfuls of cream
1 tablespoonful of brandy

Mode

Blanch and pound the almonds to a smooth paste with a smooth paste with a spoonful of water; warm the butter, mix the almonds with this and add the other ingredients, leaving out the whites of two eggs, and be particular that these are well beaten. Mix well, butter some cups, half fill them and bake the puddings from 20 minute to ½ hour. Turn them out on a dish and serve with sweet sauce.

Time

20 minutes to ½ hour.
Sufficient for four or five persons.

Bakewell Pudding I (Very Rich)

Ingredients

¼ lb of puff paste
5 eggs
6 oz of sugar
¼ lb of butter
1 oz of almonds
Jam

Mode

Cover a dish with thin puff paste, and put over this a layer of any kind of jam, ½ inch thick; put the yolks of five eggs into a basin with the white of one and beat these well; add the sifted sugar, the butter, which should be melted, and the almonds, which should be well pounded; beat all together until well mixed, then pour it into the dish over the jam and bake for an hour in a moderate oven.

Time

1 hour.
Sufficient for four or five persons.

Bakewell Pudding II

Ingredients

¾ pint of breadcrumbs
1 pint of milk
4 eggs
2 oz of sugar
3 oz of butter

1 oz of pounded almonds
Jam

Mode

Put the breadcrumbs at the bottom of a pie dish, then over them a layer of jam of any kind that may be preferred; mix the milk and eggs together; add the sugar, butter, and pounded almonds; beat all well together; pour it into the dish and bake in a moderate oven for 1 hour.

Time

1 hour.
Sufficient for four or five persons.

Baked Bread Pudding

Ingredients

½ lb of grated bread
1 pint of milk
4 eggs
4 oz of butter
4 oz of moist sugar
2 oz of candied peel
6 almonds
1 tablespoonful of brandy

Mode

Put the milk into a stewpan, with the almonds; let it infuse for ¼ hour; bring it to the boiling point; strain it onto the breadcrumbs, and let these remain till cold; then add the eggs, which should be well whisked, the butter, sugar, and brandy, and beat the pudding well until all the ingredients are thoroughly mixed, and bake for nearly ¾ hour.

Time

Nearly ¾ hour.
Sufficient for five or six persons.

Note: A few currants may be substituted for the candied peel, and will be found an excellent addition to this pudding: they should be beaten in with the mixture and not laid at the bottom of the pie dish.

Very Plain Bread Pudding

Ingredients

Odd pieces of crust or crumb of bread; to every quart allow ½ teaspoonful of salt, 1 teaspoonful of grated nutmeg, 3 oz of moist sugar, ½ lb of currants, 1½ oz of butter.

Mode

Break the bread into small pieces and pour on them as much boiling water as will soak them well. Let these stand till the water is cool; then press it out, and mash the bread with a fork until it is quite free from lumps. Measure this pulp, and to every quart stir in salt, nutmeg, sugar and currants in the above proportion; mix all well together and put it into a well-buttered pie dish. Smooth the surface with the back of a spoon, and place the butter in small pieces over the top; bake in a moderate oven for 1½ hours, and serve very hot. Boiling milk substituted for the boiling water would very much improve this pudding.

Time

1½ hours.
Sufficient for six or seven persons.

Miniature Bread Puddings

Ingredients

1 pint of milk
½ lb of breadcrumbs
4 eggs
2 oz of butter

Sugar to taste
2 tablespoonfuls of brandy
1 teaspoonful of finely minced lemon peel

Mode

Make the milk boiling, pour it onto the breadcrumbs and let them soak for about ½ hour. Beat the eggs, mix these with the breadcrumbs, add the remaining ingredients, and stir well until all is thoroughly mixed. Butter some small cups; rather more than half fill them with the mixture and bake in a moderate oven from 20 minutes to ½ hour and serve with sweet sauce. A few currants may be added to these puddings: about 3 oz will be found sufficient for the above quantity.

Time

20 minutes to ½ hour.
Sufficient for seven or eight small puddings.

Baked Bread-and-Butter Pudding

Ingredients

9 thin slices of bread and butter
1½ pints of milk
4 eggs
Sugar to taste
¼ lb of currants
Flavouring of vanilla
Grated lemon peel or nutmeg

Mode

Cut nine thin slices of bread and butter, not very thick, and put them into a pie dish, with currants between each layer and on the top. Sweeten and flavour the milk, either by infusing a little lemon peel in it or by adding a few drops of essence of vanilla; whisk the eggs well and stir these to the milk. Strain this over the bread and butter and bake in a moderate oven for 1 hour, or rather longer. This pudding may be very much enriched by adding cream, candied peel or more eggs than stated above. It should not be turned out, but sent to table in the pie dish, and is better for being made about 2 hours before it is baked.

Time

1 hour, or rather longer.
Sufficient for six or seven persons.

Royal Coburg Puddings

Ingredients

1 pint of new milk
6 oz of flour
6 oz of sugar
6 oz of butter
6 oz of currants
6 eggs
Brandy and grated nutmeg to taste

Mode

Mix the flour to a smooth batter with the milk, add the remaining ingredients *gradually*, and when well mixed, put it into four basins or moulds, half full; bake for ¾ hour, turn the puddings out on a dish, and serve with wine sauce.

Time

¾ hour.
Sufficient for seven or eight persons.

Baked Custard Pudding

Ingredients

1½ pints of milk
The rind of ¼ lemon
¼ lb of moist sugar
4 eggs

Mode

Put the milk into a saucepan with the sugar and lemon rind, and let this infuse for about ½ hour, or until the milk is well flavoured; whisk the eggs, yolks and whites; pour the milk to them, stirring all the while; then have ready a pie dish, lined at the edge with paste ready baked; strain the custard into the dish, grate a little nutmeg over the top and bake in a *very slow* oven for about ½ hour, or rather longer. The flavour of this pudding may be varied by substituting almonds for the lemon rind; and it may be very much enriched by using half cream and half milk, and doubling the quantity of eggs.

Time

½ to ¾ hour.
Sufficient for five or six persons.

Note: This pudding is usually served cold with fruit tarts.

Empress Pudding

Ingredients

½ lb of rice
2 oz of butter
3 eggs
Jam
Sufficient milk to soften the rice

Mode

Boil the rice in the milk until very soft, then add the butter. Boil it for a few minutes after the latter ingredient is put in and set it by to cool. Well beat the eggs, stir these in and line a dish with puff paste; put over this a layer of rice, then a thin layer of any kind of jam, then another layer of rice and proceed in this manner until the dish is full and bake in a moderate oven for ¾ hour. This pudding may be eaten hot or cold; if the latter, it will be much improved by having a boiled custard poured over it.

Time

¾ hour.
Sufficient for six or seven persons.

Exeter Pudding (Very Rich)

Ingredients

10 oz of breadcrumbs
4 oz of sago
7 oz of finely chopped suet
6 oz of moist sugar
The rind of ½ lemon
¼ pint of rum
7 eggs
4 tablespoonfuls of cream
4 small sponge cakes
2 oz of ratafias
Jam

Mode

Put the breadcrumbs into a basin with the sago, suet, sugar, minced lemon peel, rum and four eggs; stir these ingredients well together, then add three eggs and the cream and let the mixture be well beaten. Then butter a mould, strew in a few breadcrumbs and cover the bottom with a layer of ratafias, then put in a layer of the mixture, then a layer of sliced sponge cake spread thickly with any kind of jam; then add some ratafias, then some of the mixture and sponge cake and so on until the mould is full, taking care that a layer of the mixture is on top of the pudding. Bake in a good oven from ¾ to 1 hour and serve with the following sauce: put 3 tablespoonfuls of blackcurrant jelly into a stewpan, add two glasses of sherry and, when warm, turn the pudding out of the mould, pour the sauce over it and serve hot.

Time

From 1 to 1¼ hours.
Sufficient for seven or eight persons.

Folkestone Pudding Pies

Ingredients

1 pint of milk
3 oz of ground rice
3 oz of butter
¼ lb of sugar
Flavouring of lemon peel or bay leaf
6 eggs
Puff paste
Currants

Mode

Infuse two bay leaves, or the rind of ½ a lemon, in the milk and when it is well flavoured, strain it and add the rice; boil these for ¼ hour, stirring all the time, then take them off the fire, stir in the butter, sugar and eggs, and let these latter be well beaten before they are added to the other ingredients; when nearly cold, line some pattypans with puff paste, fill with the custard, strew over each a few currants and bake from 20 to 25 minutes in a moderate oven.

Time

20 to 25 minutes.
Sufficient to fill a dozen pattypans.

French Rice Pudding, or Gateau de Riz

Ingredients

To every ¼ lb of rice allow 1 quart* of milk, the rind of 1 lemon, ½ teaspoonful of salt, sugar to taste, 4 oz of butter, 6 eggs, breadcrumbs.

Mode

Put the milk into a stewpan with the lemon rind, and let it infuse for ½ hour or until the former is well flavoured; then take out the peel; have ready the rice washed, picked and drained; put it into the milk, and let it gradually swell over a very slow fire. Stir in the butter, salt, and sugar, and when properly sweetened, add the yolks of the eggs, and then the whites, both of which should be well beaten, and added separately to the rice. Butter a mould, strew in some fine breadcrumbs, and let them be spread equally over it; then carefully pour in the rice and bake the pudding in a slow oven for 1 hour. Turn it out of the mould and garnish the dish with preserved cherries, or any bright-coloured jelly or jam. This pudding would be exceedingly nice flavoured with essence of vanilla.

Time

¾ to 1 hour for the rice to swell; to be baked 1 hour in a slow oven.
Sufficient for five or six persons.
*[A quart is generally defined as two pints.]

Dampfnudeln or German Puddings

Ingredients

1 lb of flour
¼ lb of butter
5 eggs
2 small tablespoonfuls of yeast
2 tablespoonfuls of finely pounded sugar
Milk
A very little salt

Mode

Put the flour into a basin, make a hole in the centre, into which put the yeast and rather more than ¼ pint of warm milk; make this into a batter with the middle of the flour and let the sponge rise in a warm temperature. When sufficiently risen, mix the eggs, butter, sugar and salt with a little more warm milk and knead the whole well together with the hands, beating the dough until it is perfectly smooth and it drops from the fingers. Then cover basin with a cloth, put it in a warm place, and when the dough has nicely risen, knead it into small balls; butter the bottom of a deep sauté pan, strew over some pounded sugar and let the dampfnudeln be laid in, but do not let them touch one another, then pour over sufficient milk to cover them, put on the lid and let them rise to twice their original size by the side of the fire. Now place them in the oven for a few minutes, to acquire a nice brown colour, and serve them on a napkin, with custard sauce flavoured with vanilla or a compôte of any fruit that may be preferred.

Time

½ to ¾ hour for the sponge to rise; 10 to 15 minutes for the puddings to rise; 10 minutes to bake them in a brisk oven.
Sufficient for 10 or 12 dampfnudeln.

Baked or Boiled Ground Rice Pudding

Ingredients

2 pints of milk
6 tablespoonfuls of ground rice
Sugar to taste
4 eggs
Flavouring of lemon rind
Nutmeg
Almonds or bay leaf

Mode

Put 1½ pints of the milk into a stewpan, with any of the above flavourings, and bring it to the boiling point, and, with the other ½ pint of milk, mix the ground rice to a smooth batter; strain the boiling milk to this and stir over the fire until the mixture is tolerably thick; then pour it into a basin, leave it uncovered, and when nearly or quite cold, sweeten it to taste and add the eggs, which should be previously well beaten, with a little salt. Put the pudding into a well-buttered basin, tie it down with a cloth, plunge it into boiling water, and boil for 1½ hours. For a baked pudding, proceed in precisely the same manner, only using half the above proportion of ground rice, with the same quantity of all the other ingredients: an hour will bake the pudding in a moderate oven. Stewed fruit, or preserves, or marmalade, may be served with either the boiled or baked pudding, and will be found an improvement.

Time

1½ hours to boil; 1 hour to bake.
Sufficient for five or persons.

Manchester Pudding

Ingredients

3 oz of grated bread
½ pint of milk
A strip of lemon peel
4 eggs
2 oz of butter
Sugar to taste
Puff paste
Jam
3 tablespoonfuls of brandy

Mode

Flavour the milk with lemon peel, by infusing it in the milk for ½ hour; then strain it onto the breadcrumbs, and boil it for 2 or 3 minutes; add the eggs, leaving out the whites of two, the butter, sugar, and brandy; stir all these ingredients well together; cover a pie dish with puff paste, and at the bottom put a thick layer of any kind of jam; pour the above mixture, cold, on the jam and bake the pudding for an hour. Serve cold, with a little sifted sugar sprinkled over.

Time

1 hour.
Sufficient for five or six persons.

Sweet Macaroni Pudding

Ingredients

2½ oz of macaroni
2 pints of milk
The rind of ½ lemon
3 eggs
Sugar and grated nutmeg to taste
2 tablespoonfuls of brandy

Mode

Put the macaroni, with a pint of the milk, into a saucepan with the lemon peel, and let it simmer gently until the macaroni is tender, then put into a pie dish without the peel; mix the other pint of milk with the eggs; stir these well together, adding the sugar and brandy, and pour the mixture over the macaroni. Grate a little nutmeg over the top, and bake in a moderate oven for ½ hour. To make this pudding look nice, a paste should be laid round the edges of the dish, and, for variety, a layer of preserve or marmalade may be placed on the macaroni: in this case omit the brandy.

Time

¾ hour to simmer the macaroni; ½ hour to bake the pudding. Sufficient for five or six persons.

Manna Kroup Pudding

Ingredients

3 tablespoonfuls of manna kroup [semolina]
12 almonds
1 pint of milk
Sugar to taste
3 eggs

Mode

Blanch and pound the almonds in a mortar; mix them with the manna kroup; pour over these a pint of boiling milk and let them steep for about ¼ hour. When nearly cold, add sugar and the well-beaten eggs; mix all well together; put the pudding into a buttered dish and bake for ½ hour.

Time

½ hour.
Sufficient for four or five persons.

Mansfield Pudding

Ingredients

The crumb of 2 rolls
1 pint of milk
Sugar to taste
4 eggs
2 tablespoonfuls of brandy
6 oz of chopped suet
2 tablespoonfuls of flour
½ lb of currants
½ teaspoonful of grated nutmeg
2 tablespoonfuls of cream

Mode

Slice the roll very thin, and pour upon it a pint of boiling milk; let it remain covered close for ¼ hour, then beat it up with a fork, and sweeten with moist sugar; stir in the chopped suet, flour, currants and nutmeg. Mix these ingredients well together, moisten with the eggs, brandy, and cream; beat the mixture for 2 or 3 minutes, put it into a buttered dish or mould and bake in a moderate oven for 1¼ hours. Turn it out, strew sifted sugar over, and serve.

Time

1¼ hours.
Sufficient for six or seven persons.

Marlborough Pudding

Ingredients

¼ lb of butter
¼ lb of powdered lump sugar
4 eggs
Puff paste
A layer of any kind of jam

Mode

Beat the butter to a cream, stir in the powdered sugar, whisk the eggs, and add these to the other ingredients. When these are well mixed, line a dish with puff paste, spread over a layer of any kind of jam that may be preferred, pour in the mixture and bake the pudding for rather more than ½ hour.

Time

Rather more than ½ hour.
Sufficient for five or six persons.

Military Puddings

Ingredients

½ lb of suet
½ lb of breadcrumbs
½ lb of moist sugar
The rind and juice of 1 large lemon

Mode

Chop the suet finely, mix it with the breadcrumbs and sugar, and mince the lemon rind and strain the juice; stir these into the other ingredients, mix well, and put the mixture into small buttered cups and bake for rather more than ½ hour; turn them out on the dish and serve with lemon sauce. The above ingredients may be made into small balls and boiled for about ½ hour; they should then be served with the same sauce as when baked.

Time

Rather more than ½ hour.
Sufficient to fill six or seven moderate-sized cups.

Miniature Rice Puddings

Ingredients

¼ lb of rice
1½ pints of milk
2 oz of fresh butter
4 eggs
Sugar to taste
Flavouring of lemon peel, almonds or vanilla
A few strips of candied peel

Mode

Let the rice swell in 1 pint of the milk over a slow fire, putting with it a strip of lemon peel; stir to it the butter and the other ½ pint of milk, and let the mixture cool. Then add the well-beaten eggs and a few drops of essence of almonds or essence of vanilla, whichever may be preferred; butter well some small cups or moulds, line them with a few pieces of candied peel sliced very thin, fill them three parts full and bake for about 40 minutes; turn them out of the cups onto a white d'oyley and serve with sweet sauce. The flavouring and candied peel might be omitted and stewed fruit or preserve served instead, with these puddings.

Time

40 minutes.
Sufficient for six puddings.

Potato Pudding

Ingredients

½ lb of mashed potatoes
2 oz of butter

2 eggs
¼ pint of milk
3 tablespoonfuls of sherry
¼ saltspoonful of salt
The juice and rind of 1 small lemon
2 oz of sugar

Mode

Boil sufficient potatoes to make ½ lb when mashed; add to these the butter, eggs, milk, sherry, lemon juice, and sugar; mince the lemon peel very finely, and beat all the ingredients well together. Put the pudding into a buttered pie dish, and bake for rather more than ½ hour. To enrich it, add a few pounded almonds and increase the quantity of eggs and butter.

Time

½ hour, or rather longer.
Sufficient for five or six persons.

Quickly Made Puddings

Ingredients

¼ lb of butter
½ lb of sifted sugar
¼ lb of flour
1 pint of milk
5 eggs
A little grated lemon rind

Mode

Make the milk hot; stir in the butter, and let it cool before the other ingredients are added to it, then stir in the sugar, flour and eggs, which should be well whisked, and omit the whites of two; flavour with a little grated lemon rind and beat the mixture well. Butter some small cups, rather more than half fill them; bake from 20 minutes to ½ hour, according to the size of the puddings, and serve with fruit, custard, or wine sauce, a little of which may be poured over them.

Time

20 minutes to ½ hour.
Sufficient for six puddings.

Baked Raisin Pudding (Plain and Economical)

Ingredients

1 lb of flour
¾ lb of stoned raisins
½ lb of suet
A pinch of salt
1 oz of sugar
A little grated nutmeg
Milk

Mode

Chop the suet finely; stone the raisins and cut them in halves; mix these with the suet, add the salt, sugar and grated nutmeg and moisten the whole with sufficient milk to make it of the consistency of thick batter. Put the pudding into a buttered pie dish and bake for 1½ hours, or rather longer. Turn it out of the dish, strew sifted sugar over, and serve. This is a very plain recipe and suitable where there is a family with children. It, of course, can be much improved by the addition of candied peel, currants and rather a larger proportion of suet: a few eggs would also make the pudding richer.

Time

1½ hours.
Sufficient for seven or eight persons.

Sago Pudding

Ingredients

1½ pints of milk
3 tablespoonfuls of sago

The rind of ½ lemon
3 oz of sugar
4 eggs
1½ oz of butter
Grated nutmeg
Puff paste

Mode

Put the milk and lemon rind into a stewpan, place it by the side of the fire, and let it remain until the milk is well flavoured with the lemon, then strain it, mix with it the sago and sugar and simmer gently for about 15 minutes. Let the mixture cool a little, and stir to it the eggs, which should be well beaten, and the butter. Line the edges of a pie dish with puff paste, pour in the pudding, grate a little nutmeg over the top, and bake from ¾ to 1 hour.

Time

¾ to 1 hour, or longer if the oven is very slow.
Sufficient for five or six persons.

Baked Semolina Pudding

Ingredients

3 oz of semolina
1½ pints of milk
¼ lb of sugar
12 almonds
3 oz of butter
4 eggs

Mode

Flavour the milk with the almonds, by infusing them in it by the side of the fire for about ½ hour, then strain it and mix with it the semolina, sugar and butter. Stir these ingredients over the fire for a few minutes, then take them off and gradually mix in the eggs, which should be well beaten. Butter a pie dish, line the edges with puff paste, put in the pudding and bake in rather a slow oven from 40 to 50 minutes. Serve with custard sauce or stewed fruit, a little of which may be poured over the pudding.

Time

40 to 50 minutes.
Sufficient for five or six persons.

Somersetshire Puddings

Ingredients

3 eggs
Their weight in flour, pounded sugar and butter
Flavouring of grated lemon rind, almonds or essence of vanilla

Mode

Carefully weigh the various ingredients, by placing on one side of the scales the eggs and on the other the flour, then the sugar, and then the butter. Warm the butter and with the hands beat it to a cream; gradually dredge in the flour and pounded sugar and keep stirring and beating the mixture without ceasing until it is perfectly smooth. Then add the eggs, which should be well whisked, and either of the above flavourings that may be preferred; butter some small cups, rather more than half fill them and bake in a brisk oven for about ½ hour. Turn them out, dish them on a napkin and serve custard or wine sauce with them. A pretty little supper dish may be made of these puddings cold, by cutting out a portion of the inside with the point of a knife and putting into the cavity a little whipped cream or delicate preserve, such as apricot, greengage or very bright marmalade. The paste for these puddings requires a great deal of mixing, as the more it is beaten the better will the puddings be. When served cold, they are usually called *gâteaux à la Madeleine*.

Time

I hour.
Sufficient for six or seven puddings.

Tapioca Pudding

Ingredients

3 oz of tapioca
1 quart* of milk
2 oz of butter
¼ lb of sugar
4 eggs
Flavouring of vanilla, grated lemon rind or almonds

Mode

Wash the tapioca and let it stew gently in the milk by the side of the fire for ¼ hour, occasionally stirring it, then let it cool a little; mix with it the butter, sugar and eggs, which should be well beaten, and flavour with either of the above ingredients, putting in about twelve drops of the essence of almonds or vanilla, whichever is preferred. Butter a pie dish, and line the edges with puff paste; put in the pudding, and bake in a moderate oven for an hour. If the pudding is boiled, add a little more tapioca, and boil it in a buttered basin for 1½ hours.

Time

1 hour to bake; 1½ hours to boil.
Sufficient for five or six persons.
*[A quart is generally defined as two pints.]

Yorkshire Pudding, to Serve with Hot Roast Beef

Ingredients

1½ pints of milk
6 *large* tablespoonfuls of flour
3 eggs
1 saltspoonful of salt

Mode

Put the flour into a basin with the salt and stir gradually to this enough milk to make it into a stiff batter. When this is perfectly

YORKSHIRE PUDDING.

smooth and all the lumps are well rubbed down, add the remainder of the milk and the eggs, which should be well beaten. Beat the mixture for a few minutes and pour it into a shallow tin, which has been previously well rubbed with beef dripping. Put the pudding into the oven and bake it for 1½ hours. Cut the pudding into small square pieces, put them on a hot dish and serve. If the meat is baked, the pudding may at once be placed under it, resting the former on a small three-cornered stand.

Time

1½ hours.
Sufficient for five or six persons.

Sauces for Puddings

Arrowroot Sauce for Puddings

Ingredients

2 small teaspoonfuls of arrowroot
4 dessertspoonfuls of pounded sugar
The juice of 1 lemon
¼ teaspoonful of grated nutmeg
½ pint of water

Mode

Mix the arrowroot smoothly with the water; put this into a stewpan; add the sugar, strained lemon juice and grated nutmeg. Stir these ingredients over the fire until they boil, when the sauce is ready for use. A small quantity of wine, or any liqueur, would very much improve the flavour of this sauce: it is usually served with bread, rice, custard, or any dry pudding that is not very rich.

Time

Altogether, 15 minutes.
Sufficient for six or seven persons.

Sago Sauce for Sweet Puddings

Ingredients

1 tablespoonful of sago
⅓ pint of water
¼ pint of port or sherry
The rind and juice of 1 small lemon
Sugar to taste
When the flavour is liked, a little pounded cinnamon.

Mode

Wash the sago in two or three waters, then put it into a saucepan, with the water and lemon peel; let it simmer gently by the fire for 10 minutes; then take out the lemon peel, add the remaining ingredients, give one boil, and serve. Be particular to strain the lemon juice before adding it to the sauce. This, on trial, will be found a delicious accompaniment to various boiled puddings, such as those made of bread, raisins, rice, etc.

Time

10 minutes.
Sufficient for seven or eight persons.

Sweet Sauce for Puddings

Ingredients

½ pint of melted butter made with milk
3 heaped teaspoonfuls of pounded sugar
Flavouring of grated lemon rind, or nutmeg, or cinnamon

Mode

Make ½ pint of melted butter, omitting the salt; stir in the sugar, add a little grated lemon rind, nutmeg or powdered cinnamon and serve. Previously to making the melted butter, the milk can be flavoured with almonds, by infusing about half a dozen of them in it for about ½ hour; the milk should then be strained before it is added to the other ingredients. This simple sauce may be served for children with rice, batter or bread pudding.

Time

Altogether, 15 minutes.
Sufficient for six or seven persons.

Vanilla Custard Sauce, to Serve with Puddings

Ingredients

½ pint of milk
2 eggs
2 oz of sugar
10 drops of essence of vanilla

Mode

Beat the eggs, sweeten the milk; stir these ingredients well together and flavour them with essence of vanilla, regulating the proportion of this latter ingredient by the strength of the essence, the size of the eggs, etc. Put the mixture into a small jug, place this jug in a saucepan of boiling water and stir the sauce *one way* until it thickens, but do not allow it to boil or it will instantly curdle. Serve in a boat or tureen separately, with plum, bread or any kind of dry pudding. Essence of almonds or lemon rind may be substituted for the vanilla, when they are more in accordance with the flavouring the pudding with which the sauce is intended to be served.

Time

To be stirred in the jug from 8 to 10 minutes.
Sufficient for four or five persons.

An Excellent Wine Sauce for Puddings

Ingredients

The yolks of 4 eggs
1 teaspoonful of flour
2 oz of pounded sugar
2 oz of fresh butter
¼ saltspoonful of salt
½ pint of sherry or Madeira

Mode

Put the butter and flour into a saucepan and stir them over the fire until the former thickens; then add the sugar, salt, and wine, and mix these ingredients well together. Separate the yolks from the whites of four eggs; beat up the former and stir them briskly to the sauce; let it remain over the fire until it is on the point of simmering; but do not allow it to boil, or it will instantly curdle. This sauce is delicious with plum, marrow or bread puddings; but should be served separately and not poured over the pudding.

Time

From 5 to 7 minutes to thicken the butter; about 5 minutes to stir the sauce over the fire.
Sufficient for seven or eight persons.

Wine or Brandy Sauce for Puddings

Ingredients

½ pint of melted butter
3 heaped teaspoonfuls of pounded sugar
1 *large* wineglassful of port or sherry, or ¾ of a *small* glassful of brandy

Mode

Make ½ pint of melted butter, omitting the salt, then stir in the sugar and wine, or spirit, in the above proportion and bring the sauce to the point of boiling. Serve in a boat or tureen separately, and, if liked, pour a little of it over the pudding. To convert this into punch sauce, add to the sherry and brandy a small wineglassful of rum and the juice and grated rind of ½ lemon. Liqueurs, such as Maraschino or Curaçao, substituted for the brandy, make excellent sauces.

Time

Altogether, 15 minutes.
Sufficient for six or seven persons.

Wine Sauce for Puddings

Ingredients

½ pint of sherry
¼ pint of water
The yolks of 5 eggs
2 oz of pounded sugar
½ teaspoonful of minced lemon peel
A few pieces of candied citron cut thin

Mode

Separate the yolks from the whites of five eggs; beat them and put them into a very clean saucepan (if at hand, a lined one is best); add all the other ingredients, place them over a sharp fire and keep stirring until the sauce begins to thicken, then take it off and serve. If it is allowed to boil, it will be spoiled, as it will immediately curdle.

Time

To be stirred over the fire 3 or 4 minutes, but it must not boil.
Sufficient for a large pudding; allow half this quantity for a moderate-sized one.

Miscellaneous

Almond Puffs

Ingredients

2 tablespoonfuls of flour
2 oz of butter

2 oz of pounded sugar
2 oz of sweet almonds

Mode

Blanch and pound the almonds in a mortar to a smooth paste; melt the butter, dredge in the flour and add the sugar and pounded almonds. Beat the mixture well and put it into cups or very tiny jelly pots, which should be well buttered, and bake in a moderate oven for about 20 minutes, or longer should the puffs be large. Turn them out on a dish, the bottom of the puff uppermost and serve.

Time

20 minutes.
Sufficient for two or three persons.

Baked Beef I

Ingredients

About 2 lbs of cold roast beef
2 small onions
1 large carrot or two small ones
1 turnip
A small bunch of savoury herbs
Salt and pepper to taste
4 tablespoonfuls of gravy
3 tablespoonfuls of ale
Crust or mashed potatoes

Mode

Cut the beef in slices, allowing a small amount of fat to each slice; place a layer of this in the bottom of a pie dish, with a portion of the onions, carrots, and turnips, which must be sliced; mince the herbs, strew them over the meat, vegetables, and seasoning; and proceed in this manner until all the ingredients are used. Pour in the gravy and ale (water may be substituted for the former, but it is not so nice), cover with a crust or mashed potatoes, and bake for ½ hour, or rather longer.

Time

Rather more than ½ hour.
Sufficient for five or six persons.

Note: It is as well to parboil the carrots and turnips before adding them to the meat and to use some of the liquor in which they were boiled as a substitute for gravy; that is to say, when there is no gravy at hand. Be particular to cut the onions in *very thin* slices.

Baked Beef II

Ingredients

Slices of cold roast beef
Salt and pepper to taste
1 sliced onion
1 teaspoonful of minced savoury herbs
5 or 6 tablespoonfuls of gravy or sauce of any kind
Mashed potatoes

Mode

Butter the sides of a deep dish and spread mashed potatoes over the bottom of it; on this, place layers of beef in thin slices (this may be minced if there is not sufficient beef to cut into slices), well seasoned with pepper and salt and a very little onion and herbs, which should be previously fried of a nice brown, then put another layer of mashed potatoes, and beef, and other ingredients, as before; pour in the gravy or sauce, cover the whole with another layer of potatoes, and bake for ½ hour. This may be served in the dish or turned out.

Time

½ hour.

Sufficient

A large pie dish full for five or six persons.

Biscuit Powder (Generally used for Infants' Food)

This powder may be purchased in tin canisters, and may also be prepared at home. Dry the biscuits well in a slow oven; roll them and grind them with a rolling pin on a clean board, until they are reduced to powder; sift it through a close hair sieve, and it is fit for use. It should be kept in well covered tins and in a dry place.

Chocolate Soufflé

Ingredients

4 eggs
3 teaspoonfuls of pounded sugar
1 teaspoonful of flour
3 oz of the best chocolate

Mode

Break the eggs, separating the whites from the yolks, and put them into different basins; add to the yolks the sugar, flour and chocolate, which should be very finely grated, and stir these ingredients for 5 minutes. Then well whisk the whites of the eggs in the other basin, until they are stiff, and, when firm, mix lightly with the yolks, till the whole forms a smooth and light substance; butter a round cake tin, put in the mixture and bake in a moderate oven from 15 to 20 minutes. Pin a white napkin round the tin, strew sifted sugar over the top of the soufflé and send it immediately to table. The proper appearance of this dish depends entirely on the expedition with which it is served, and some cooks, to preserve lightness, hold a salamander over the soufflé until it is placed on the table. If allowed to stand after it comes from the oven, it will entirely spoil, as it falls almost immediately.

Time

15 to 20 minutes.
Sufficient for a moderate-sized soufflé.

To Bake a Ham

Ingredients

Ham
A common crust

Mode

As a ham for baking should be well soaked, let it remain in water for at least 12 hours. Wipe it dry, trim away any rusty places underneath and cover it with a common crust, taking care that this is of sufficient thickness all over to keep the gravy in. Place it in a moderately heated oven and bake for nearly 4 hours. Take off the crust, and skin, and cover with raspings [breadcrumbs], the same as for boiled ham, and garnish the knuckle with a paper frill. This method of cooking a ham is, by many persons, considered far superior to boiling it, as it cuts fuller of gravy and has a finer flavour, besides keeping a much longer time good.

Time

A medium-sized ham, 4 hours.

Meringues

Ingredients

½ lb of pounded sugar
The whites of 4 eggs

Mode

Whisk the whites of the eggs to a stiff froth and, with a wooden spoon, stir in quickly the pounded sugar, and have some boards thick enough to put in the oven to prevent the bottom of the meringues from acquiring too much colour. Cut some strips of paper about 2 inches wide; place this paper on the board and drop a tablespoonful at a time of the mixture on the paper, taking care to let all the meringues be the same size. In dropping it from the spoon, give the mixture the form of an egg, and keep the meringues about 2 inches apart from each other on the paper. Strew over them some sifted sugar, and bake in a moderate oven for ½ hour. As soon as they begin to colour, remove them from the oven; take each slip of paper by the two ends, and turn it gently on the table and, with a small spoon, take out the soft part of each meringue. Spread some clean paper on the board, turn the meringues upside down and put them into the oven to harden and brown on the other side. When required for table, fill them with whipped cream, favoured with liqueur or vanilla and sweetened with pounded sugar. Join two of the meringues together and pile them high in the dish. To vary their appearance, finely chopped almonds or currants may be strewn over them before the sugar is sprinkled over and they may be garnished with any bright-coloured preserve. Great expedition is necessary in making this sweet dish; as, if the meringues are not put into the oven as soon as the sugar and eggs are mixed, the former melts and the mixture would run on the paper, instead of keeping its egg shape. The sweeter the meringues are made, the crisper will they be, but, if there is not sufficient sugar mixed with them, they will most likely be tough. They are sometimes coloured; and if kept well covered in a dry place, will remain good for a month or six weeks.

Time

Altogether, about ½ hour.
Sufficient to make two dozen meringues.

Baked Minced Mutton

Ingredients

The remains of any joint of cold roast mutton
1 or 2 onions
1 bunch of savoury herbs
Pepper and salt to taste
2 blades of pounded mace or nutmeg
2 tablespoonfuls of gravy
Mashed potatoes

Mode

Mince an onion rather fine and fry it a light brown colour; add the herbs and mutton, both of which should be also finely minced and well mixed; season with pepper and salt and a little pounded mace or nutmeg and moisten with the above proportion of gravy. Put a layer of mashed potatoes at the bottom of a dish, then the mutton, and then another layer of potatoes, and bake for about ½ hour.

Time

½ hour.

Note: If there should be a large quantity of meat, use two onions instead of one.

Baked Potatoes

Ingredients

Potatoes

Mode

Choose large potatoes, as much of a size as possible; wash them in lukewarm water and scrub them well, for the browned skin of a baked potato is by many persons considered the better part of it. Put them into a moderate oven and bake them for about 2 hours, turning them three or four times whilst they are cooking. Serve them in a napkin immediately they are done, as, if kept a long time in the oven, they have a shrivelled appearance. Potatoes may also be roasted in front of the fire, in an American oven; but when thus cooked, they must be done very slowly. Do not forget to send to table with them a piece of cold butter.

Time

Large potatoes, in a hot oven, 1½ hours to 2 hours; in a cool oven, 2 to 2½ hours.
Sufficient: Allow two to each person.

BAKED POTATOES SERVED IN NAPKIN.

Potato Pasty

Ingredients

1½ lbs of rump steak or mutton cutlets
Pepper and salt to taste
⅓ pint of weak broth or gravy
1 oz of butter
Mashed potatoes

Mode

Place the meat, cut in small pieces, at the bottom of the pan; season it with pepper and salt and add the gravy and butter broken into small pieces. Put on the perforated plate, with its valve pipe screwed on, and fill up the whole space to the top of the tube with nicely mashed potatoes mixed with a little milk, and finish the surface of them in any ornamental manner. If carefully baked, the potatoes will be covered with a delicate brown crust, retaining all the savoury steam rising from the meat. Send it to table as it comes from the oven, with a napkin folded round it.

Time

40 to 60 minutes.
Sufficient for four or five persons.

Potted Lobsters

Ingredients

2 lobsters
Seasoning to taste, of nutmeg, pounded mace, white pepper and salt
¼ lb of butter
3 or 4 bay leaves

Mode

Take out the meat carefully from the shell but do not cut it up. Put some butter at the bottom of a dish, lay in the lobster as evenly as possible, with the bay leaves and seasoning between. Cover with butter and bake for ¾ hour in a gentle oven. When done, drain the whole on a sieve, and lay the pieces in potting jars, with the seasoning about them. When cold, pour over it clarified butter, and, if very highly seasoned, it will keep some time.

Time

¾ hour.

Note: Potted lobster may be used cold or as a *fricassee* with cream sauce.

Rice Soufflé

Ingredients

3 tablespoonfuls of ground rice
1 pint of milk
5 eggs
Pounded sugar to taste
Flavouring of lemon rind, vanilla, coffee, chocolate, or anything that may be preferred
A piece of butter the size of a walnut

Mode

Mix the ground rice with 6 tablespoonfuls of the milk quite smoothly, and put it into a saucepan with the remainder of the milk and butter and keep stirring it over the fire for about ¾ hour, or until the mixture thickens. Separate the yolks from the whites of the eggs, beat the former in a basin and stir to them the rice and sufficient pounded sugar to sweeten the soufflé, but add this latter ingredient as sparingly as possible, as the less sugar there is used, the lighter will be the soufflé. Now whisk the whites of the eggs to a stiff froth or snow; mix them with the other preparation, and pour the whole into a soufflé dish and put it instantly into the oven; bake it about ½ hour in a moderate oven; take it out, hold a salamander over the top, sprinkle sifted sugar over it, and send the soufflé to table in the dish it was baked in, either with a napkin pinned round or inclosed in a more ornamental dish. The excellence of this fashionable dish entirely depends on the proper whisking of the whites of the eggs, the manner of baking, and the expedition with which it is sent to table. Soufflés should be served instantly from the oven, or they will sink and be nothing more than an ordinary pudding.

Time

About ½ hour.
Sufficient for three or four persons.

To Make a Soufflé

Ingredients

3 heaped tablespoonfuls of potato flour, rice flour, arrowroot, or tapioca
1 pint of milk
5 eggs
A piece of butter the size of a walnut
Sifted sugar to taste
¼ saltspoonful of salt
Flavouring

Mode

Mix the potato flour, or whichever one of the above ingredients is used, with a little of the milk; put it into a saucepan, with the remainder of the milk, the butter, salt, and sufficient pounded sugar to sweeten the whole nicely. Stir these ingredients over the fire until the mixture thickens; then take it off the fire, and let it cool a little. Separate the whites from the yolks of the eggs, beat the latter, and stir them into the soufflé batter. Now whisk the whites of the eggs to the firmest possible froth, for on this depends the excellence of the dish; stir them to the other ingredients, and add a few drops of essence of any flavouring that may be preferred; such as vanilla, lemon, orange, ginger, etc. Pour the batter into a soufflé dish, put it immediately into the oven, and bake for about ½ hour, then take it out, put the dish into another more ornamental one, such as is made for the purpose; hold a salamander over the soufflé, strew it with sifted sugar, and send it instantly to table. The secret of making a soufflé well is to have the eggs well whisked, but particularly the whites, the oven not too hot, and to send it to table the moment it comes from the oven. If the soufflé be ever so well made, and it is allowed to stand before being sent to table, its appearance and goodness will be entirely spoiled. Soufflés may be flavoured in various ways, but must be named accordingly. Vanilla is one of the most delicate and recherché flavourings that can be used for this very fashionable dish.

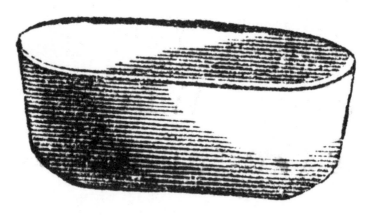

SOUFFLE-PAN.

Time

About ½ hour in the oven; 2 or 3 minutes to hold the salamander over.
Sufficient for three or four persons.

Savoury Casserole of Rice, or Rice Border, for Ragouts, Fricassées, etc. (an Entrée)

Ingredients

1½ lbs of rice
3 pints of weak stock or broth
2 slices of fat ham
1 teaspoonful of salt

Mode

A casserole of rice, when made in a mould, is not such a difficult operation as when it is moulded by the hand. It is an elegant and inexpensive entrée, as the remains of cold fish, flesh or fowl may be served as ragoûts, fricassées, etc., inclosed in the casserole. It requires great nicety in its preparation, the principal thing to attend to being the boiling of the rice, as, if this is not sufficiently cooked, the casserole, when moulded, will have a rough appearance, which would entirely spoil it. After having washed the rice in two or three waters, drain it well and put it into a stewpan with the stock, ham, and salt; cover the pan closely, and let the rice gradually swell over a slow fire, occasionally stirring, to prevent its sticking. When it is quite soft, strain it, pick out the pieces of ham and, with the back of a large wooden spoon, mash the rice to a perfectly smooth paste. Then grease a mould well (moulds are made purposely for rice borders) and turn it upside down for a minute or two, to drain away the fat, should there be too much; put some rice all round the bottom and sides of it; place a piece of soft bread in the middle and cover it with rice; press it in equally with the spoon, and let it cool. Then dip the mould into hot water, turn the casserole carefully onto a dish, mark where the lid is to be formed on the top, by making an incision with the point of a knife about an inch from the edge all round and put it into a *very hot* oven. Brush it over with a little clarified butter and bake for about ½ hour, or rather longer, then carefully remove the lid, which will be formed by the incision having been made all round, and remove the bread, in small pieces, with the point of a knife, being careful not to injure the casserole. Fill the centre with the ragoût or fricassée, which should be made thick; put on the cover, glaze it, place it in the oven to set the glaze and serve as hot as possible. The casserole should not be emptied too much, as it is liable to crack from the weight of whatever is put in, and in baking it, let the oven be very hot or the casserole will probably break.

Time

About ¾ hour to swell the rice.
Sufficient for two moderate-sized casseroles.

Toad-in-the-Hole (a Homely but Savoury Dish)

Ingredients

1½ lbs of rump steak
1 sheep's kidney
Pepper and salt to taste.

For the batter:
3 eggs
1 pint of milk
4 tablespoonfuls of flour
½ saltspoonful of salt

Mode

Cut up the steak and kidney into convenient-sized pieces and put them into a pie dish, with a good seasoning of salt and pepper; mix the flour with a small quantity of milk at first, to prevent its being lumpy; add the remainder, and the 3 eggs, which should be well beaten; put in the salt, stir the batter for about 5 minutes, and pour it over the steak. Place it in a tolerably brisk oven immediately and bake for 1½ hours.

Time

1½ hours.
Sufficient for four or five persons.

Note: The remains of cold beef, rather underdone, may be substituted for the steak and, when liked, the smallest possible quantity of minced onion or shalot may be added.

Toad-in-the-Hole (with Mutton)

Ingredients

6 oz of flour
1 pint of milk
3 eggs
Butter
A few slices of cold mutton
Pepper and salt to taste
2 kidneys

Mode

Make a smooth batter of flour, milk and eggs in the above proportion; butter a baking dish and pour in the batter. Into this, place a few slices of cold mutton, previously well seasoned, and the kidneys, which should be cut into rather small pieces; bake for about 1 hour, or rather longer, and send it to table in the dish it was baked in. Oysters or mushrooms may be substituted for kidneys, and will be found exceedingly good.

Time

Rather more than 1 hour.

Baking With the Seasons

Times When Things are in Season

January

Fish – Barbel, brill, carp, cod, crabs, crayfish, dace, eels, flounders, haddocks, herrings, lampreys, lobsters, mussels, oysters, perch, pike, plaice, prawns, shrimps, skate, smelts, soles, sprats, sturgeon, tench, thornback, turbot, whitings.
Meat – Beef, house lamb, mutton, pork, veal, venison.
Poultry – Capons, fowls, tame pigeons, pullets, rabbits, turkeys.
Game – Grouse, hares, partridges, pheasants, snipe, wild-fowl, woodcock.
Vegetables – Beetroot, broccoli, cabbages, carrots, celery, chervil, cresses, cucumbers (forced), endive, lettuces, parsnips, potatoes, savoys, spinach, turnips, various herbs.
Fruit – Apples, grapes, medlars, nuts, oranges, pears, walnuts, crystallised preserves (foreign), dried fruits, such as almonds and raisins; French and Spanish plums; prunes, figs, dates.

February

Fish – Barbel, brill, carp, cod may be bought, but is not so good as in January, crabs, crayfish, dace, eels, flounders, haddocks, herrings, lampreys, lobsters, mussels, oysters, perch, pike, plaice, prawns, shrimps, skate, smelts, soles, sprats, sturgeon, tench, thornback, turbot, whiting.
Meat – Beef, house lamb, mutton, pork, veal.

Poultry – Capons, chickens, ducklings, tame and wild pigeons, pullet with eggs, turkeys, wild fowl, though now not in full season.

Game – Grouse, hares, partridges, pheasants, snipes, woodcock.

Vegetables – Beetroot, broccoli (purple and white), Brussels sprouts, cabbages, carrots, celery, chervil, cresses, cucumbers (forced), endive, kidney beans, lettuces, parsnips, potatoes, savoys, spinach, turnips, various herbs.

Fruit – Apples (golden and Dutch pippins), grapes, medlars, nuts, oranges, pears (Bon Chrétien), walnuts, dried fruits (foreign), such as almonds and raisins; French and Spanish plums; prunes, figs, dates, crystallised preserves.

March

Fish – Barbel, brill, carp, crabs, crayfish, dace, eels, flounders, haddocks, herrings, lampreys, lobsters, mussels, oysters, perch, pike, plaice, prawns, shrimps, skate, smelts, soles, sprats, sturgeon, tench, thornback, turbot, whiting.

Meat – Beef, house lamb, mutton, pork, veal.

Poultry – Capons, chickens, ducklings, tame and wild pigeons, pullets with eggs, turkeys, wild fowl, though now not in full season.

Game – Grouse, hares, partridges, pheasants, snipes, woodcock.

Vegetables – Beetroot, broccoli (purple and white), Brussels sprouts, cabbages, carrots, celery, chervil, cresses, cucumbers (forced), endive, kidney beans, lettuces, parsnips, potatoes, savoys, sea kale, spinach, turnips, various herbs.

Fruit – Apples (golden and Dutch pippins), grapes, medlars, nuts, oranges, pears (Bon Chrétien), walnuts, dried fruits (foreign), such as almonds and raisins; French and Spanish plums; prunes, figs, dates, crystallised preserves.

April

Fish – Brill, carp, cockles, crabs, dory, flounders, ling, lobsters, red and grey mullet, mussels, oysters, perch, prawns, salmon (but rather scarce and expensive), shad, shrimps, skate, smelts, soles, tench, turbot, whitings.

Meat – Beef, lamb, mutton, veal.

Poultry – Chickens, ducklings, fowls, leverets, pigeons, pullets, rabbits.

Game – Hares.

Vegetables – Broccoli, celery, lettuces, young onions, parsnips, radishes, small salad, sea kale, spinach, sprouts, various herbs.

Fruit – Apples, nuts, pears, forced cherries, etc., for tarts, rhubarb, dried fruits, crystallised preserves.

May

Fish – Carp, chub, crabs, crayfish, dory, herrings, lobsters, mackerel, red and grey mullet, prawns, salmon, shad, smelts, soles, trout, turbot.

Meat – Beef, lamb, mutton, veal.

Poultry – Chickens, ducklings, fowls, green geese, leverets, pullets, rabbits.

Vegetables – Asparagus, beans, early cabbages, carrots, cauliflowers, cresses, cucumbers, lettuces, pease, early potatoes, salads, sea kale, various herbs.

Fruit – Apples, green apricots, cherries, currants for tarts, gooseberries, melons, pears, rhubarb, strawberries.

June

Fish – Carp, crayfish, herrings, lobsters, mackerel, mullet, pike, prawns, salmon, soles, tench, trout, turbot.

Meat – Beef, lamb, mutton, veal, buck venison.

Poultry – Chickens, ducklings, fowls, green geese, leverets, plovers, pullets, rabbits, turkey poults, wheatears.

Vegetables – Artichokes, asparagus, beans, cabbages, carrots, cucumbers, lettuces, onions, parsnips, pease, potatoes, radishes, small salads, sea kale, spinach, various herbs.

Fruit – Apricots, cherries, currants, gooseberries, melons, nectarines, peaches, pears, pineapples, raspberries, rhubarb, strawberries.

July

Fish – Carp, crayfish, dory, flounders, haddocks, herrings, lobsters, mackerel, mullet, pike, plaice, prawns, salmon, shrimps, soles, sturgeon, tench, thornback.

Meat – Beef, lamb, mutton, veal, buck venison.

Poultry – Chickens, ducklings, fowls, green geese, pigeons, plovers, pullets, rabbits, turkey poults, wheatears, wild ducks (called flappers).

Game – Leverets, grouse, blackcock.

Vegetables – Artichokes, asparagus, beans, carrots, cabbages, cauliflowers, celery, cresses, endive, lettuces, mushrooms, onions, pease, potatoes, radishes, sea kale, small salading, sprouts, turnips, various kitchen herbs, vegetable marrows.

Fruit – Apricots, cherries, currants, figs, gooseberries, melons, nectarines, pears, pineapples, plums, raspberries, strawberries, walnuts in high season and pickled.

August

Fish – Brill, carp, cub, crayfish, crabs, dory, eels, flounders, grigs, herrings, lobsters, mullet, pike, prawns, salmon, shrimps, skate, soles, sturgeon, thornback, trout, turbot.

Meat – Beef, lamb, mutton, veal, buck venison.

Poultry – Chickens, ducklings, fowls, green geese, pigeons, plovers, pullets, rabbits, turkey poults, wheatears, wild ducks.

Game – Leverets, grouse, blackcock.

Vegetables – Artichokes, asparagus, beans, carrots, cabbages, cauliflowers, celery, cresses, endive, lettuces, mushrooms, onions, pease, potatoes, radishes, sea kale, small salading, sprouts, turnips, various kitchen herbs, vegetable marrows.

Fruit – Currants, figs, filberts, gooseberries, grapes, melons, mulberries, nectarines, peaches, pears, pineapples, plums, raspberries, walnuts.

September

Fish – Brill, carp, cod, eels, flounders, lobsters, mullet, oysters, plaice, prawns, skate, soles, turbot, whiting, whitebait.

Meat – Beef, lamb, mutton, pork, veal.

Poultry – Chickens, ducks, fowls, geese, larks, pigeons, pullets, rabbits, teal, turkeys.

Game – Blackcock, buck venison, grouse, hares, partridges, pheasants.

Vegetables – Artichokes, asparagus, beans, cabbage sprouts, carrots, celery, lettuces, mushrooms, onions, pease, potatoes, salading, sea kale, sprouts, tomatoes, turnips, vegetable marrows, various herbs.

Fruit – Bullaces, damsons, figs, filberts, grapes, melons, morella cherries, mulberries, nectarines, peaches, pears, plums, quinces, walnuts.

October

Fish – Barbel, brill, cod, crabs, eels, flounders, gudgeons, haddocks, lobsters, mullet, oysters, plaice, prawns, skate, soles, tench, turbot, whiting.

Meat – Beef, mutton, pork, veal, venison.

Poultry – Chickens, fowls, geese, larks, pigeons, pullets, rabbits, teal, turkeys, widgeons, wild ducks.

Game – Blackcock, grouse, hares, partridges, pheasants, snipes, woodcocks, doe venison.

Vegetables – Artichokes, beets, cabbages, cauliflowers, carrots, celery, lettuces, mushrooms, onions, potatoes, sprouts, tomatoes, turnips, vegetable marrows, various herbs.

Fruit – Apples, black and white bullaces, damsons, figs, filberts, grapes, pears, quinces, walnuts.

November

Fish – Brill, carp, cod, crabs, eels, gudgeons, haddocks, oysters, pike, soles, tench, turbot, whiting.

Meat – Beef, mutton, veal, doe venison.

Poultry – Chickens, fowls, geese, larks, pigeons, pullets, rabbits, teal, turkeys, widgeons, wild duck.

Game – Hares, partridges, pheasants, snipes, woodcocks.

Vegetables – Beetroot, cabbages, carrots, celery, lettuces, late cucumbers, onions, potatoes, salading, spinach, sprouts, various herbs.

Fruit – Apples, bullaces, chestnuts, filberts, grapes, pears, walnuts.

December

Fish – Barbel, brill, carp, cod, crabs, eels, dace, gudgeons, haddocks, herrings, lobsters, oysters, perch, pike, shrimps, skate, sprats, soles, tench, thornback, turbot, whiting.

Meat – Beef, house lamb, mutton, pork, venison.
Poultry – Capons, chickens, fowls, geese, pigeons, pullets, rabbits, teal, turkeys, widgeons, wild ducks.
Game – Hares, partridges, pheasants, snipes, woodcocks.
Vegetables – Broccoli, cabbages, carrots, celery, leeks, onions, potatoes, parsnips, Scotch kale, turnips, winter spinach.
Fruit – Apples, chestnuts, filberts, grapes, medlars, oranges, pears, walnuts, dried fruits, such as almonds and raisins, figs, dates, etc., crystallised preserves.

Spring

Lemons

The lemon is a variety of the citron. The juice of this fruit makes one of our most popular and refreshing beverages – lemonade, which is gently stimulating and cooling and soon quenches the thirst. It may be freely partaken by bilious and sanguine temperaments; but persons with irritable stomachs should avoid it, on account of its acid qualities. The fresh rind of the lemon is a gentle tonic and, when dried and grated, is used in flavouring a variety of culinary preparations. Lemons appear in company with the orange in most orange-growing countries. They were only known to the Romans at a very late period, and, at first, were used only to keep the moths from their garments: their acidity was unpleasant to them. In the time of Pliny, the lemon was hardly known otherwise than as an excellent counter-poison.

Lemon Cake

Ingredients

10 eggs
3 tablespoonfuls of orange flower water
¾ lb of pounded loaf sugar
1 lemon
¾ lb of flour

Mode

Separate the whites from the yolks of the eggs; whisk the former to a stiff froth; add the orange flower water, the sugar, grated lemon rind and mix these ingredients well together. Then beat the yolks of the eggs, and add them, with the lemon juice, to the whites, etc.; dredge in the flour gradually, keep beating the mixture well, put it into a buttered mould and bake the cake about an hour, or rather longer. The addition of a little butter, beaten to a cream, we think, would improve this cake.

Time

About 1 hour.

Lemon Cheesecakes

Ingredients

¼ lb of butter
1 lb of loaf sugar
6 eggs
The rind of 2 lemons and the juice of 3

Mode

Put all the ingredients into a stewpan, carefully grating the lemon rind and straining the juice. Keep stirring the mixture over the fire until the sugar is dissolved and it begins to thicken: when of the consistency of honey, it is done, then put it into small jars and keep in a dry place. When made into cheesecakes, add a few pounded almonds, or candied peel, or grated sweet biscuit; line some pattypans with good puff paste, rather more than half fill them with the mixture and bake for about ¼ hour in a good brisk oven.

Time

¼ hour.
Sufficient for twenty-four cheesecakes.

Baked Lemon Pudding I

Ingredients

The yolks of 4 eggs
4 oz of pounded sugar
1 lemon
¼ lb of butter
Puff crust

Mode

Beat the eggs to a froth; mix with them the sugar and warmed butter; stir these ingredients well together, putting in the grated rind and strained juice of the lemon. Line a shallow dish with puff paste; put in the mixture and bake in a moderate oven for 40 minutes; turn the pudding out of the dish, strew over it sifted sugar, and serve.

Time

40 minutes
Sufficient for five or six persons.

Baked Lemon Pudding II

Ingredients

10 oz of breadcrumbs
2 pints of milk
2 oz of butter
1 lemon
¼ lb of pounded sugar
4 eggs
1 tablespoonful of brandy

Mode

Bring the milk to the boiling point, stir in the butter, and pour these hot over the breadcrumbs; add the sugar and very finely minced lemon peel; beat the eggs, and stir these in with the brandy to the other ingredients; put a paste round the dish and bake for ¾ hour.

Time

¾ hour.
Sufficient for six or seven persons.

Baked Lemon Pudding III (Very Rich)

Ingredients

The rind and juice of 2 large lemons
½ lb of loaf sugar
¼ pint of cream
The yolks of 8 eggs
2 oz of almonds
½ lb of butter, melted

Mode

Mix the pounded sugar with the cream, and add the yolks
of eggs and the butter, which should be previously warmed.
Blanch and pound the almonds and put these, with the grated
rind and strained juice of the lemons, to the other ingredients.
Stir all well together; line a dish with puff paste, put in the
mixture and bake for 1 hour.

Time

1 hour.
Sufficient for six or seven persons.

Lemon Sauce for Sweet Puddings

Ingredients

The rind and juice of 1 lemon
1 tablespoonful of flour
1 oz of butter
1 wineglassful of sherry
1 wineglassful of water
Sugar to taste
The yolks of 4 eggs

Mode

Rub the rind of the lemon on to some lumps of sugar; squeeze out the juice and strain it; put the butter and flour into a saucepan, stir them over the fire and when of a pale brown, add the wine, water, and strained lemon juice. Crush the lumps of sugar that were rubbed on the lemon; stir these into the sauce, which should be very sweet. When these ingredients are well mixed, and the sugar is melted, put in the beaten yolks of 4 eggs; keep stirring the sauce until it thickens, when serve. Do not, on any account, allow it to boil, or it will curdle, and be entirely spoiled.

Time

Altogether, 15 minutes.
Sufficient for seven or eight persons.

Rhubarb

This is one of the most useful of all garden productions that are put into pies and puddings. It was comparatively little

RHUBARB.

known till within the last twenty or thirty years, but it is now cultivated in almost every British garden. The part used is the footstalks of the leaves, which, peeled and cut into small pieces, are put into tarts, either mixed with apples or alone. When quite young, they are much better not peeled. Rhubarb comes in season when apples are going out. The common rhubarb is a native of Asia; the scarlet variety has the finest flavour. Turkey rhubarb, the well-known medicinal drug, is the root of a very elegant plant (*Rheum palmatum*), coming to greatest perfection in Tartary. For culinary purposes, all kinds of rhubarb are the better for being blanched.

Rhubarb Tart

Ingredients

½ lb of puff paste
About 5 sticks of large rhubarb
¼ lb of moist sugar

Mode

Make a medium puff crust by the recipe on page 108; line the edges of a deep pie dish with it and wash, wipe and cut the rhubarb into pieces about 1 inch long. Should it be old and tough, string it, that is to say, pare off the outside skin. Pile the fruit high in the dish as it shrinks very much in the cooking; put in the sugar, cover with crust, ornament the edges and bake the tart in a well-heated oven from ½ to ¾ hour. If wanted very nice, brush it over with the white of an egg beaten to a stiff froth, then sprinkle on it some sifted sugar and put it in the oven just to set the glaze: this should be done when the tart is nearly baked. A small quantity of lemon juice and a little of the peel minced, are by many persons considered an improvement to the flavour of rhubarb tart.

Time

½ to ¾ hour.
Sufficient for four or five persons.

Veal

Baked Veal

Ingredients

½ lb of cold roast veal
A few slices of bacon

1 pint of breadcrumbs
½ pint of good veal gravy
½ teaspoonful of minced lemon peel
1 blade of pounded mace
Cayenne and salt to taste
4 eggs

Mode

Mince finely the veal and bacon; add the breadcrumbs, gravy and seasoning and stir these ingredients well together. Beat up the eggs thoroughly; add these, mix the whole well together, put into a dish and bake from ¾ to 1 hour. When liked, a little good gravy may be served in a tureen as an accompaniment.

Time

From ¾ to 1 hour.
Sufficient for three or four persons.

Veal Olive Pie

Ingredients

A few thin slices of cold fillet of veal
A few thin slices of bacon
Forcemeat*
A cupful of gravy
4 tablespoonfuls of cream
Puff crust

Mode

Cut thin slices from a fillet of veal, place on them thin slices of bacon, and over them, a layer of forcemeat, with an additional seasoning of shallot and cayenne; roll them tightly, and fill up a pie dish with them; add the gravy and cream, cover with a puff crust, and bake for 1 to 1½ hour: should the pie be very large, allow 2 hours. The pieces of rolled veal should be about 3 inches in length and about 3 inches round.

Time

Moderate-sized pie, 1 to 1½ hours.
Sufficient for four persons.
*[Forcemeat for a pie like this would consist of bacon, suet, lemon rind, salt, cayenne, mace, breadcrumbs and eggs.]

Veal Pie

Ingredients

2 lbs of veal cutlets
1 or 2 slices of lean bacon or ham
Pepper and salt to taste
2 tablespoonfuls of minced savoury herbs
2 blades of pounded mace
Crust
1 teacupful of gravy

Mode

Cut the cutlets into square pieces and season them with pepper, salt and pounded mace; put them in a pie dish with the savoury herbs sprinkled over, and one or two slices of lean bacon or ham placed at the top: if possible, this should be previously cooked, as undressed bacon makes the veal red, and spoils it in any way that is approved; brush it over with the yolk of an egg, and bake in a well-heated oven for about 1½ hours. Pour in a good gravy after baking, which is done by removing the top ornament, and replacing it after the gravy is added.

Time

About 1½ hours.
Sufficient for five or six persons.

Veal and Ham Pie

Ingredients

2 lbs of veal cutlets
½ lb of boiled ham

2 tablespoonfuls of minced savoury herbs
¼ teaspoonful of grated nutmeg
2 blades of pounded mace
Pepper and salt to taste
A strip of lemon peel, finely minced
The yolks of 2 hard-boiled eggs
½ pint of water
Nearly ½ pint of good strong gravy
Puff crust

Mode

Cut the veal into nice square pieces and put a layer of them at the bottom of a pie dish; sprinkle over these a portion of the herbs, spices, seasoning, lemon peel, and the yolks of the eggs cut in slices; cut the ham very thin and put a layer of this in. Proceed in this manner until the dish is full, so arranging it that the ham comes at the top. Lay a puff paste on the edge of the dish and pour in about ½ pint of water; cover with crust, ornament it with leaves, brush it over with the yolk of an egg, and bake in a well-heated oven for 1 to 1½ hours, or longer, should the pie be very large. When it is taken out of the oven, pour in at the top, through a funnel, nearly ½ pint of strong gravy: this should be made sufficiently good that, when cold, it may cut in a firm jelly. This pie may be very much enriched by adding a few mushrooms, oysters or sweetbreads, but it will be found very good without any of the last-named additions.

Time

1½ hours, or longer, should the pie be very large.
Sufficient for five or six persons.

Raised Pie of Veal and Ham

Ingredients

3 or 4 lbs of veal cutlets
A few slices of bacon or ham
Seasoning of pepper, salt, nutmeg and allspice
Forcemeat*

2 lbs of hot-water paste
½ pint of good strong gravy

Mode

RAISED PIE.

To raise the crust for a pie with the hands is a very difficult task and can only be accomplished by skilled and experienced cooks. The process should be seen to be satisfactorily learnt and plenty of practice given to the making of raised pies, as by that means only will success be insured. Make a hot-water paste, and from the mass raise the pie with the hands; if this cannot be accomplished, cut out pieces for the top and bottom and a long piece for the sides; fasten the bottom and side pieces together by means of egg and pinch the edges well together then line the pie with forcemeat, put in a layer of veal and a plentiful seasoning of salt, pepper, nutmeg, nutmeg, and allspice, as, let it be remembered, these pies taste very insipid unless highly seasoned. Over the seasoning, place a layer of sliced bacon or cooked ham and then a layer of forcemeat, veal, seasoning, and bacon, and so on until the meat rises to about an inch above the paste, taking care to finish with a layer of forcemeat, to fill all the cavities of the pie and to lay in the meat firmly and compactly. Brush the top edge of the pie with beaten egg, put on the cover, press the edges, and pinch them round with paste pincers. Make a hole in the middle of the lid and ornament the pie with leaves, which should be stuck on with the white of an egg, then brush it all over with the beaten yolk of an egg and bake the pie in an oven with a soaking heat from 3 to 4 hours. To ascertain when it is done, run a sharp-pointed knife or skewer through the hole at the top into the middle of the pie, and if the meat feels tender, it is sufficiently baked**. Have ready about ½ pint of very strong gravy, pour it through a funnel into the hole at the top, stop up the hole with a small leaf of baked paste and put the pie away until wanted for use. Should it acquire too much colour in the baking, cover it with paper, as the crust should not in the least degree be burnt. Mushrooms, truffles and many other ingredients may be added to enrich the flavour of these pies, and the very fleshy parts of the meat may be larded. These pies are more frequently served cold than hot and form excellent dishes for cold suppers or breakfasts. The cover of the pie is sometimes carefully removed, leaving the perfect edges and the top decorated with square pieces of very bright aspic jelly: this has an exceedingly pretty effect.

Time

About 4 hours.
Sufficient for a very large pie.
*[Forcemeat for a pie like this would consist of bacon, suet, lemon rind, salt, cayenne, mace, breadcrumbs and eggs.]
**[Always ensure meat is thoroughly cooked and piping hot before serving.]

Summer

Cherries

According to Lucullus, the cherry tree was known in Asia in the year of Rome 680. Seventy different species of cherries, wild and cultivated, exist, which are distinguishable from each other by the difference of their form, size and colour. The French distil from cherries a liqueur named *kirsch-waser* (*eau de cérises*); the Italians prepare, from a cherry called marusca, the liqueur named

marasquin, sweeter and more agreeable than the former. The most wholesome cherries have a tender and delicate skin; those with a hard skin should be very carefully masticated. Sweetmeats, syrups, tarts, entremets, etc., of cherries are universally approved.

Cherry Tart

Ingredients

1½ lbs of cherries
2 small tablespoonfuls of moist sugar
½ lb of short crust

CHERRY.

Mode

Pick the stalks from the cherries, put them, with the sugar, into a deep pie dish just capable of holding them, with a small cup placed upside down in the midst of them. Make a shortcrust with ½ lb of flour by one of the recipes included earlier in this book; lay a border round the edge of the dish; put on the cover and ornament the edges; bake in a brisk oven from ½ hour to 40 minutes; strew finely sifted sugar over and serve hot or cold, although the latter is the more usual mode. It is more economical to make two or three tarts at one time, as the trimmings from one tart answer for lining the edges of the dish for another, and so much paste is not required as when they are made singly. Unless for family use, never make fruit pies in very large dishes; select them, however, as deep as possible.

Time

½ hour to 40 minutes.
Sufficient for five or six persons.

Note: A few currants added to the cherries will be found to impart a nice piquant taste to them.

Cherry Sauce for Sweet Puddings (German Recipe)

Ingredients

1 lb of cherries
1 tablespoonful of flour
1 oz butter
½ pint of water
1 wineglassful of port wine
A little grated lemon rind
4 pounded cloves
2 tablespoonfuls of lemon juice
Sugar to taste

Mode

Stone the cherries; put the butter and flour into a saucepan; stir them over the fire until of a pale brown; then add the cherries, the wine, and the water. Simmer these gently for ¼ hour, or until the cherries are quite cooked, and rub the whole through a hair sieve; add the remaining ingredients, let the sauce boil for another 5 minutes, and serve.

Time

20 minutes to ½ hour.
Sufficient for four or five persons.

Eel

The Common Eel: This fish is known frequently to quit its native element and to set off on a wandering expedition in the night, or just about the close of day, over the meadows, in search of snails and other prey. It also, sometimes, betakes itself to isolated ponds, apparently for no other pleasure than that which may be supposed to be found in a change of habitation. This, of course, accounts for eels being found in waters which were never suspected to contain them. This rambling disposition in the eel has been long known to naturalists and, from the following lines, it seems to have been known to the ancients: 'Thus the mail'd tortoise, and the wand'ring eel. Oft to the neighbouring beach will silent steal'.

THE EEL.

Eel Pie

Ingredients

1 lb of eels
A little chopped parsley
1 shalot
Grated nutmeg

Pepper and salt to taste
The juice of ½ a lemon
Small quantity of forcemeat
¼ pint of béchamel
Puff paste

Mode

Skin and wash the eels, cut them into pieces 2 inches long, and line the bottom of the pie dish with forcemeat. Put in the eels, and sprinkle them with the parsley, shalots, nutmeg, seasoning and lemon juice and cover with puff paste. Bake for 1 hour, or rather more; make the bechamel hot and pour it into the pie.

Time

Rather more than 1 hour.

Gooseberries

The red and the white are the two principal varieties of gooseberries. The red are rather more acid; but, when covered with white sugar, are most wholesome, because the sugar neutralises their acidity. Red gooseberries make an excellent jelly, which is light and refreshing, but not very nourishing. It is good for bilious and plethoric persons and to invalids generally who need light and digestible food. It is a fruit from which many dishes might be made. All sorts of gooseberries are agreeable when stewed, and, in this country especially, there is no fruit so universally in favour. In Scotland, there is scarcely a cottage garden

THE GOOSEBERRY.

without its gooseberry bush. Several of the species are cultivated with the nicest care.

Baked Gooseberry Pudding

Ingredients

1½ pints of gooseberries
3 eggs
1½ oz of butter
½ pint of breadcrumbs
Sugar to taste

Mode

Put the gooseberries into a jar, previously cutting off the tops and tails; place this jar in boiling water and let it boil until the gooseberries are soft enough to pulp, then beat the through a coarse sieve, and to every pint of pulp add 3 well-whisked eggs, 1½ oz of butter, ½ pint of breadcrumbs and sugar to taste; beat the mixture well, put a border of puff paste round the edge of a pie dish, put in the pudding, bake for about 40 minutes, strew sifted sugar over and serve.

Time

About 40 minutes.
Sufficient for four or five persons.

Gooseberry Tart

Ingredients

1½ pints of gooseberries
½ lb of shortcrust (see page 123, 'Another Good Short Crust')
¼ lb of moist sugar

Mode

With a pair of scissors cut off the tops and tails of the gooseberries; put them into a deep pie dish, pile the fruit high in the centre and put in the sugar; line the edge of the dish with short crust, put on the cover, and ornament the edges; bake in a good oven for about ¾ hour, and before being sent to table, strew over it some finely sifted sugar. A jug of cream, or a dish of boiled or baked custards, should always accompany this dish.

Time

¾ hour.
Sufficient for five or six persons.

Mackerel

The Mackerel: This is not only one of the most elegantly formed, but one of the most beautifully coloured fishes, when taken out of the sea, that we have. Death, in some degree, impairs the vivid splendour of its colours, but it does not entirely obliterate them. It visits the shores of Great Britain in countless shoals, appearing about March, off the Land's End; in the bays of Devonshire, about April; off Brighton in the beginning of May and on the coast of Suffolk about the beginning of June. In the Orkneys they are seen till August, but the greatest fishery is on the west coasts of England.

To Choose Mackerel: In choosing this fish, purchasers should, to a great extent, be regulated by the brightness of its appearance. If it have a transparent, silvery hue, the flesh is good, but if it be red about the head, it is stale.

THE MACKEREL.

Baked Mackerel

Ingredients

4 middling-sized mackerel
A nice delicate forcemeat*
3 oz of butter
Pepper and salt to taste

Mode

Clean the fish, take out the roes, and fill up with forcemeat and sew up the slit**. Flour, and put them in a dish, heads and tails alternately, with the roes. Between each layer, put some little pieces of butter, and pepper and salt. Bake for ½ hour, and either serve with plain melted butter or a *maître d'hôtel* sauce.

Time

½ hour.
Sufficient for six persons.
*[Forcemeat for this dish would consist of butter, suet, bacon, herbs, onion, salt, nutmeg, cayenne, breadcrumbs and egg.]
**[Today we would probably not sew up the fish.]

Pineapple

Pineapple Chips

Ingredients

Pineapples
Sugar to taste

Mode

Pare and slice the fruit thinly, put it on dishes, and strew over it plenty of pounded sugar. Keep it in a hot closet, or very slow oven, eight or ten days, and turn the fruit every day until dry, then put the pieces of pineapple on tins, and place them in a quick oven for 10 minutes. Let them cool, and store them away in dry boxes, with paper between each layer.

Time

Eight to ten days.

Raspberries

There are two sorts of raspberries, the red and the white. Both the scent and flavour of this fruit are very refreshing, and the berry itself is exceedingly wholesome and invaluable to people of a nervous or bilious temperament. We are not aware, however, of its being cultivated with the same amount of care which is bestowed upon some other of the berry tribe, although it is far from improbable that a more careful cultivation would not be repaid by a considerable

RASPBERRY.

improvement in the size and flavour of the berry; neither, as an eating fruit, is it so universally esteemed as the strawberry, with whose lusciousness and peculiarly agreeable flavour it can bear no comparison. In Scotland, it is found in large quantities, growing wild, and is eagerly sought after, in the woods, by children. Its juice is rich and abundant and, to many, extremely agreeable.

Red Currant and Raspberry Tart

Ingredients

1½ pints of picked currants
½ pint of raspberries
3 heaped tablespoonfuls of moist sugar
½ lb of shortcrust (see page 123)

Mode

Strip the currants from the stalks and put them into a deep pie dish, with a small cup placed in the midst, bottom upwards; add the raspberries and sugar; place a border of paste round the edge of the dish, cover with crust, ornament the edges and bake from ½ to ¾ hour; strew some sifted sugar over before being sent to table. This tart is more generally served cold than hot.

Time

½ to ¾ hour.
Sufficient for five or six persons.

Sea Bream

This is an abundant fish in Cornwall and it is frequently found in the fish market of Hastings during the summer months, but is not in much esteem.

Baked Sea Bream

Ingredients

1 bream
Seasoning to taste of salt, pepper and cayenne
¼ lb of butter

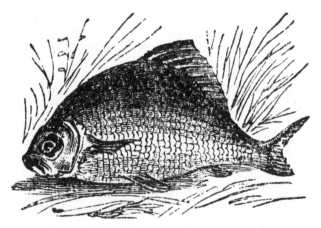

THE SEA-BREAM.

Mode

Well wash the bream, but do not remove the scales, and wipe away all moisture with a nice dry cloth. Season it inside and out with salt, pepper, and cayenne, and lay it in a baking dish. Place the butter, in small pieces, upon the fish, and bake for rather more than ½ hour. To stuff this fish before baking will be found a great improvement.

Time

Rather more than ½ hour.

Strawberries

The name of this favourite fruit is said to be derived from an ancient custom of putting straw beneath the fruit when it began to ripen, which is very useful to keep it moist and clean. The strawberry belongs to temperate and rather cold climates, and no fruit of these latitudes that ripens without the aid of artificial heat is at all comparable with it in point of flavour. The strawberry is widely diffused, being found in most parts of the world, particularly in Europe and America.

Among the Greeks, the name of the strawberry indicated its tenuity, this fruit forming hardly a mouthful. With the Latins, the name reminded one of the delicious perfume of this plant. Both nations were equally fond of it and applied the same care to its cultivation. Virgil appears to place it in the same rank with flowers, and Ovid gives it a tender epithet, which delicate palates would not disavow. Neither does this luxurious poet forget the wild strawberry, which disappears beneath its modest foliage, but whose presence the scented air reveals.

Open Tart of Strawberry or any other kind of preserve

Ingredients

Trimmings of puff paste
Any kind of jam

Mode

Butter a tart pan; roll out the paste to the thickness of ½ inch and line the pan with it; prick a few holes at the bottom with a fork and bake the tart in a brisk oven from 10 to 15 minutes. Let the paste cool a little; then fill it with preserve, place a few stars or leaves on it, which have been previously cut out of the paste and baked, and the tart is ready for the table. By making it in this manner, both the flavour and colour of the jam are preserved, which would otherwise be lost, were it baked in the oven on the paste, and, besides, so much jam is not required.

Time

10 to 15 minutes.
Sufficient: one tart for three persons.

Vol-au-Vent of Fresh Strawberries with Whipped Cream

Ingredients

¾ lb of puff paste (see page 107)
1 pint of freshly gathered strawberries
Sugar to taste
A plateful of whipped cream

Mode

Make a vol-au-vent case by the recipe on page 122, only not quite so large nor so high as for a savoury one. When nearly done, brush the paste over with the white of an egg, then sprinkle on it some pounded sugar and put it back in the oven to set the glaze. Remove the interior, or soft crumb and, at the moment of serving, fill it with the strawberries, which should be picked and broken up with sufficient sugar to sweeten them nicely. Place a few spoonfuls of whipped cream on the top and serve.

Time

½ hour to 40 minutes to bake the vol-au-vent.
Sufficient for one vol-au-vent.

Sweetbreads

Baked Sweetbreads

Ingredients

3 sweetbreads
Egg and breadcrumbs
Oiled butter
3 slices of toast
Brown gravy

Mode

Choose large white sweetbreads; put them into warm water to draw out the blood and to improve their colour; let them remain for rather more than 1 hour, then put them into boiling water and allow them to simmer for about 10 minutes, which renders them firm. Take them up, drain them, brush over the egg, sprinkle with breadcrumbs; dip them in egg again and then into more breadcrumbs. Drop on them a little oiled butter, and put the sweetbreads into a moderately heated oven and let them bake for nearly ¾ hour. Make three pieces of toast; place the sweetbreads on the toast and pour round, but not over them, a good brown gravy.

Time

To soak 1 hour, to be boiled 10 minutes, baked 40 minutes. Sufficient for an entrée.

SWEETBREADS.

Tomatoes

The tomato is a native of tropical countries but is now cultivated considerably both in France and England. Its skin is of a brilliant red, and its flavour, which is somewhat sour, has become of immense importance in the culinary art. It is used both fresh and preserved. When eaten fresh, it is served as an entremets; but its principal use is in sauce and gravy; its flavour stimulates the appetite and is almost universally approved. The Tomato is a wholesome fruit and digests easily. From July to September, they gather the tomatoes green in France, not breaking them away from the stalk; they are then hung, head downwards, in a dry and not too cold place and there they ripen.

Baked Tomatoes (Excellent)

Ingredients

8 or 10 tomatoes
Pepper and salt to taste
2 oz of butter
Breadcrumbs

Mode

Take off the stalks from the tomatoes; cut them into thick slices and put them into a deep baking dish; add a plentiful seasoning of pepper and salt and butter in the above proportion; cover the whole with bread crumbs; drop over these a little clarified butter; bake in a moderate oven from 20 minutes to ½ hour and serve very hot. This vegetable, dressed as above, is an exceedingly nice accompaniment to all kinds of roast meat. The tomatoes, instead of being cut in slices, may be baked whole, but they will take rather longer time to cook.

Time

20 minutes to 1 hour.
Sufficient for five or six persons.

Autumn

Apples

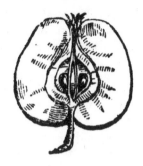

The most useful of all the British fruits is the apple, which is a native of Britain, and may be found in woods and hedges in the form of the common wild crab, of which all our best apples are merely seminal varieties, produced by culture or particular circumstances. In most temperate climates, it is very extensively cultivated, and in England, both as regards variety and quantity, it is excellent and abundant. Immense supplies are also imported from the United States and France. The apples grown in the vicinity of New York are universally admitted to be the finest of any, but unless selected and packed with great care, they are apt to spoil before reaching England.

This useful fruit is mentioned in Holy Writ and Homer describes it as valuable in his time. It was brought from the East by the Romans, who held it in the highest estimation. Indeed, some of the citizens of the 'Eternal City' distinguished certain favourite apples by their names. Thus the Manlians were called after Manlius, the Claudians after Claudius and the Appians after Appius. Others were designated after the country hence they were brought; as the Sidonians, the Epirotes and the Greeks. The best varieties are native of Asia and have, by grafting them upon others, been introduced into Europe. The crab, found in our hedges, is the only variety indigenous to Britain; therefore, for the introduction of other kinds, we are, no doubt, indebted to the Romans. In the time of the Saxon heptarchy, both Devon and Somerset were distinguished as *the apple country*, and there are still existing in Herefordshire some trees said to have been planted in the time of William the Conqueror. From that time to this, the varieties of this precious fruit have gone on increasing and are now said to number upwards of 1,500. It is peculiar to the temperate zone, being found neither in Lapland, nor within the tropics. The best baking apples for early use are the Colvilles; the best for autumn are the Rennets and Pearmains; and the best for winter and spring are Russets. The best table, or eating, apples are the Margarets for early use; the Kentish Codlin and summer Pearmain for summer, and for autumn, winter or spring, the Dowton, golden and other pippins, as the Ribstone, with small Russets. As a food, the apple cannot be considered to rank high, as more than the half of it consists of water and the rest of its properties are not the most nourishing. It is, however, a useful adjunct to other kinds of food, and, when cooked, is esteemed as slightly laxative.

No fruit is so universally popular as the apple. It is grown extensively for cider, but many sorts are cultivated for the table. The apple, uncooked, is less digestible than the pear; the degree of digestibility varying according to the firmness of texture and flavour. Very wholesome and delicious jellies, marmalades and sweetmeats are prepared from it. Entremets of apples are made in great variety. Apples, when peeled, cored, and well cooked, are a grateful food for the dyspeptic.

Uses of the Apple: It is well known that this fruit forms a very important article of food, in the form of pies and puddings, and furnishes several delicacies, such as sauces, marmalades, and jellies, and is much esteemed as a dessert fruit. When flattened in the form of round cakes, and baked in ovens, they are called beefings, and large quantities are annually dried in the sun in America, as well as in Normandy, and stored for use during winter, when they may be stewed or made into pies. In a roasted state, they are remarkably wholesome and, it is said, strengthening to a weak stomach. In putrid and malignant fevers, when used with the juice of lemons and currants, they are considered highly efficacious.

Constituents of the Apple: All apples contain sugar, malic acid or the acid of apples; mucilage or gum; woody fibre, and water; together with some aroma, on which their peculiar flavour depends. The hard acid kinds are unwholesome if eaten raw, but by the process of cooking, a great deal of this acid is decomposed and converted into sugar. The sweet and mellow kinds form a valuable addition to the dessert. A great part of the acid juice is converted into sugar as the fruit ripens, and even after it is gathered, by a natural process, termed maturation, but, when apples decay, the sugar is changed into a bitter principle and the mucilage becomes mouldy and offensive. Old cheese has a remarkable effect in meliorating the apple when eaten; probably from the volatile alkali or ammonia of the cheese neutralising its acid.

To Preserve Apples: The best mode of preserving apples is to carry them at once to the fruit room, where they should be put upon shelves, covered with white paper, after gently wiping each of the fruit. The room should be dry, and well aired, but should not admit the sun. The finer and larger kinds of fruit should not be allowed to touch each other but should be kept separate. For this purpose, a number of shallow trays should be provided, supported by racks or stands above each other. In very cold frosty weather, means should be adopted for warming the room.

Apple Cheesecakes

Ingredient

½ lb of apple pulp
¼ lb of sifted sugar
¼ lb of butter
4 eggs
The rind and juice of 1 lemon

Mode

Pare, core and boil sufficient apples to make ½ lb when cooked; add to these the sugar, the butter, which should be melted, the eggs, leaving out two of the whites, and the grated rind and juice of one lemon; stir the mixture well; line some pattypans with puffpaste, put in the mixture and bake for about 20 minutes.

Time

About 20 minutes.
Sufficient for about eighteen or twenty cheesecakes.

Apple Soufflé

Ingredients

6 oz of rice
1 quart* of milk
The rind of ½ lemon
Sugar to taste
The yolks of 4 eggs
The whites of 6
1½ oz of butter
4 tablespoonfuls of apple marmalade

Mode

Boil the milk with the lemon peel until the former is well flavoured, then strain it, put in the rice and let it gradually swell over a slow fire, adding sufficient sugar to sweeten it nicely. Then crush the rice to a smooth pulp with the back of a wooden spoon; line the bottom and sides of a round cake tin with it and put it into the oven to set; turn it out of the tin carefully, and be careful that the border of rice is firm in every part. Mix with the marmalade the beaten yolks of eggs and the butter and stir these over the fire until the mixture thickens. Take it off the fire; to this, add the whites of the eggs, which should be previously beaten to a strong froth; stir all together and put it into the rice border. Bake in a moderate oven for about ½ hour, or until the soufflé rises very light. It should be watched and served instantly, or it will immediately fall after it is taken from the oven.

Time

½ hour.
Sufficient for four or five persons.
*[A quart is generally defined as two pints.]

Thick Apple Jelly or Marmalade, for Entremets or Dessert Dishes

Ingredients

Apples; to every lb of pulp allow ¾ lb of sugar, ½ teaspoonful of minced lemon peel.

Mode

Peel, core and boil the apples with only sufficient water to prevent them from burning; beat them to a pulp, and to every lb of pulp, allow the above proportion of sugar in lumps. Dip the lumps into water; put these into a saucepan and boil till the syrup is thick and can be well skimmed; then add this syrup to the apple pulp, with the minced lemon peel, and stir it over a quick fire for about 20 minutes, or until the apples cease to stick to the bottom of the pan. The jelly is then done and may be poured into moulds which have been previously dipped in water, when it will turn out nicely for dessert or a side dish; for the latter, a little custard should be poured round and it should be garnished with strips of citron or stuck with blanched almonds.

Time

½ to ¾ hour to reduce the apples to a pulp; 20 minutes to boil after the sugar is added.
Sufficient: 1½ lb of apples for a small mould.

Apple Tart or Pie

Ingredients

Puff paste (see the recipe on page 108 or 109), apples; to every lb of unpared apples allow 2 oz of moist sugar, ½ teaspoonful of finely minced lemon peel, 1 tablespoonful of lemon juice.

Mode

Make ½ lb of puff paste by either of the above-named recipes, place a border of it round the edge of a pie dish and fill it with apples pared, cored, and cut into slices; sweeten with moist sugar, add the lemon peel and juice and 2 or 3 tablespoonfuls of water; cover with crust, cut it evenly round close to the edge of the pie dish and bake in a hot oven from ½ to ¾ hour, or rather longer, should the pie be very large. When it is three parts done, take it out of the oven, put the white of an egg on a plate and, with the blade of a knife, whisk it to a froth; brush the pie over with this, then sprinkle upon it some sifted sugar and then a few drops of water. Put the pie back into the oven, and finish baking, and be particularly careful that it does not catch or burn, which it is very liable to do after the crust is iced. If made with a plain crust, the icing may be omitted.

Time

½ hour before the crust is iced; 10 to 15 minutes afterwards.

Sufficient

Allow 2 lbs of apples for a tart for six persons.

Note: Many things are suggested for the flavouring of apple pie; some say 2 or 3 tablespoonfuls of beer, others the same quantity of sherry, which very much improve the taste, whilst the old fashioned addition of a few cloves is, by many persons, preferred to anything else, as also a few slices of quince.

Baked Apple Custard

Ingredients

1 dozen large apples
Moist sugar to taste
1 small teacupful of cold water
The grated rind of 1 lemon
1 pint of milk
4 eggs
2 oz of loaf sugar

Mode

Peel, cut, and core the apples; put them into a lined saucepan with the cold water, and as they heat, bruise them to a pulp; sweeten with moist sugar, and add the grated lemon rind. When cold, put the fruit at the bottom of a pie dish, and pour over it a custard, made with the above proportion of milk, eggs and sugar; grate a little nutmeg over the top, place the dish in a moderate oven and bake from 25 to 35 minutes. The above proportions will make rather a large dish.

Time

25 to 35 minutes.
Sufficient for six or seven persons.

Charlotte-aux-Pommes

Ingredients

A few slices of rather stale bread ½ inch thick
Clarified butter
Apple marmalade made by the recipe on page 201, with about 2 dozen apples
½ glass of sherry

Mode

Cut a slice of bread the same shape as the bottom of a plain round mould, which has been well buttered, and a few strips the height of the mould, and about 1½ inches wide; dip the bread in clarified butter (or spread it with cold butter, if not wanted quite so rich); place the round piece at the bottom of the mould and set the narrow strips up the sides of it, overlapping each other a little, that no juice from the apples may escape, and that they may hold firmly to the mould. Brush the interior over with the white of egg (this will assist to make the case firmer); fill it with apple marmalade made by the recipe on page 201, with the addition of a little sherry, and cover them with a round piece of bread, also brushed over with egg, the same as the bottom; slightly press the bread

CHARLOTTE-AUX-POMMES.

down to make it adhere to the other pieces; put a plate on the top and bake the charlotte, in a brisk oven, of a light colour. Turn it out on the dish, strew sifted sugar over the top, and pour round it a little melted apricot jam.

Time

40 to 50 minutes.
Sufficient for five or six persons.

An Easy Method of Making a Charlotte-aux-Pommes

Ingredients

½ lb of flour
¼ lb of butter
¼ lb of powdered sugar
½ teaspoonful of baking powder
1 egg
Milk
1 glass of raisin wine
Apple marmalade (see page 201)
¼ pint of cream

2 dessertspoonfuls of pounded sugar
2 tablespoonfuls of lemon juice

Mode

Make a cake with the flour, butter, sugar, and baking powder; moisten with the egg and sufficient milk to make it the proper consistency, and bake it in a round tin. When cold, scoop out the middle, leaving a good thickness all round the sides, to prevent them breaking; take some of the scooped-out pieces, which should be trimmed into neat slices; lay them in the cake, and pour over sufficient raisin wine, with the addition of a little brandy, if approved, to soak them well. Have ready some apple marmalade, made by the recipe on page 201; place a layer of this over the soaked cake, then a layer of cake and a layer of apples; whip the cream to a froth, mixing with it the sugar and lemon juice; pile it on the top of the charlotte, and garnish it with pieces of clear apple jelly. This dish is served cold, but may be eaten hot, by omitting the cream, and merely garnishing the top with bright jelly just before it is sent to table.

Time

1 hour to bake the cake.
Sufficient for five or six persons.

A Very Simple Apple Charlotte

Ingredients

9 slices of bread and butter
About 6 good-sized apples
1 tablespoonful of minced lemon peel
2 tablespoonfuls of juice
Moist sugar to taste

Mode

Butter a pie dish; place a layer of bread and butter, without the crust, at the bottom; then a layer of apples, pared, cored and cut into thin slices; sprinkle over these a portion of the lemon peel and juice and sweeten with moist sugar. Place another layer of bread and butter, and then one of apples, proceeding in this manner until the dish is full; then cover it up with the peel of the apples, to preserve the top from browning or burning; bake in a brisk oven for rather more than ¾ hour; turn the charlotte on a dish, sprinkle sifted sugar over and serve.

Time

¾ hour.
Sufficient for five or six persons.

Creamed Apple Tart

Ingredients

Puff crust (see recipes on pages 108 and 109)
To every lb of pared and cored apples, allow 2 oz moist sugar, ½ teaspoonful of minced lemon peel, 1 tablespoonful of lemon juice, ½ pint of boiled custard.

Mode

Make an apple tart by the recipe on pages 201–2, with the exception of omitting the icing. When the tart is baked, cut out the middle of the lid or crust, leaving a border all round the dish. Fill up with a nicely made boiled custard, grate a little nutmeg over the top, and the pie is ready for table. This tart is usually eaten cold; it is rather an old fashioned dish, but, at the same time, extremely nice.

Time

½ to ¾ hour.
Sufficient for five or six persons.

Apple Tourte or Cake (German Recipe)

Ingredients

10 or 12 apples
Sugar to taste
The rind of 1 small lemon

3 eggs
¼ pint of cream or milk
¼ lb of butter
¾ lb of good short crust (see recipe on page 123)
3 oz of sweet almonds

Mode

Pare, core and cut the apples into small pieces; put sufficient moist sugar to sweeten them into a basin; add the lemon peel, which should be finely minced, and the cream; stir these ingredients well, whisk the eggs and melt the butter; mix altogether, add the sliced apple, and let these be well stirred into the mixture. Line a large round plate with the paste, place a narrow rim of the same round the outer edge, and lay the apples thickly in the middle. Blanch the almonds, cut them into long shreds and strew over the top of the apples, and bake from ½ to ¾ hour, taking care that the almonds do not get burnt; when done, strew some sifted sugar over the top and serve. This tourte may be eaten either hot or cold and is sufficient to fill two large-sized plates.

Time

½ to ¾ hour.
Sufficient for two large-sized tourtes.

Baked Apple Dumplings (a Plain Family Dish)

Ingredients

6 apples
¾ lb of suet crust from the recipe on page 126
Sugar to taste

Mode

Pare and take out the cores of the apples without dividing them and make ½ lb of suet crust; roll the apples in the crust, previously sweetening them with moist sugar, and taking care to join the paste nicely. When they are formed into round balls, put them on a tin and bake them for about ½ hour, or longer should the apples be very large; arrange them pyramidically on a dish, and sift over them some pounded white sugar. These may be made richer by using one of the puff pastes instead of suet.

Time

From ½ to ¾ hour, or longer.
Sufficient for four persons.

Baked Apple Pudding

Ingredients

5 moderate-sized apples
2 tablespoonfuls of finely chopped suet
3 eggs
3 tablespoonfuls of flour
1 pint of milk
A little grated nutmeg

Mode

Mix the flour to a smooth batter with the milk; add the eggs, which should be well whisked, and put this batter into a well-buttered pie dish. Wipe the apples clean, but do not pare them; cut them in halves and take out the cores; lay them in the batter, rind uppermost; shake the suet on the top, over which also grate a little nutmeg; bake in a moderate oven for an hour and cover, when served, with sifted loaf sugar. This pudding is also very good with the apples pared, sliced and mixed with the batter.

Time

1 hour.
Sufficient for five or six persons.

Flanc of Apples, or Apples in a Raised Crust (Sweet Entremets)

Ingredients

¾ lb of short crust (see page 123)
9 moderate-sized apples

The rind and juice of ½ lemon
½ lb of white sugar
¾ pint of water
A few strips of candied citron

Mode

Make a short crust by either of the above recipes; roll it out
to the thickness of ½ inch and butter an oval mould; line it
with the crust and press it carefully all round the sides, to
obtain the form of the mould, but be particular not to break
the paste. Pinch the part that just rises above the mould with
the paste pincers and fill the case with flour; bake it for about
1 hour, then take it out of the oven, remove the flour, put the
case back in the oven for another ¼ hour, and do not allow it
to get scorched. It is now ready for the apples, which should
be prepared in the following manner; peel, and take out the
cores with a small knife, or a cutter for the purpose, without
dividing the apples; put them into a small lined saucepan, just
capable of holding them, with sugar, water, lemon juice and
rind, in the above proportion. Let them simmer very gently
until tender; then take out the apples, let them cool, arrange
them in the flanc or case, and boil down the syrup until
reduced to a thick jelly; pour it over the apples and garnish
them with a few slices of candied citron.

Another flanc may be made by rolling out the paste, cutting
the bottom of a round or oval shape and then a narrow strip for
the sides: these should be stuck on with the white of an egg, to
the bottom piece, and the flanc then filled with raw fruit, with
sufficient sugar to sweeten it nicely. It will not require so long
baking as in a mould, but the crust must be made everywhere of
an equal thickness, and so perfectly joined, that the juice does not
escape. This dish may also be served hot, and should be garnished
in the same manner, or a little melted apricot jam may be poured
over the apples, which very much improves their flavour.

Time

Altogether, 1 hour to bake the flanc, from 30 to 40 minutes to
stew the apples very gently.
Sufficient for one entremets or side dish.

Rich Baked Apple Pudding

Ingredients

½ lb of the pulp of apples
½ lb of loaf sugar
6 oz of butter
The rind of 1 lemon
6 eggs
Puff paste

Mode

Peel, core and cut the apples, as for sauce; put them into a stewpan, with only just sufficient water to prevent them from burning, and let them stew until reduced to a pulp. Weigh the pulp, and to every ½ lb add sifted sugar, grated lemon rind and six well-beaten eggs. Beat these ingredients well together, then melt the butter, stir it to the other things, put a border of puff paste round the dish and bake for rather more than ½ hour. The butter should not be added until the pudding is ready for the oven.

Time

½ to ¾ hour.
Sufficient for five or six persons.

Rich Baked Apple Pudding II (More Economical)

Ingredients

12 large apples
6 oz of moist sugar
¼ lb butter
4 eggs
1 pint of breadcrumbs

Mode

Pare, core and cut the apples, as for sauce, and boil them until reduced to a pulp, then add the butter, melted and the eggs, which should be well whisked. Beat up the pudding for 2 or 3 minutes;

butter a pie dish; put in a layer of bread crumbs, then the apple and then another layer of breadcrumbs; flake over these a few tiny pieces of butter and bake for about ½ hour.

Time

About ½ hour.
Sufficient for five or six persons.

Note: A very good economical pudding may be made merely with apples, boiled and sweetened, with the addition of a few strips of lemon peel. A layer of bread crumbs should be placed above and below the apples, and the pudding baked for ½ hour.

Apricot

The apricot is indigenous to the plains of Armenia, but is now cultivated in almost every climate, temperate or tropical. There are several varieties. The skin of this fruit has a perfumed flavour, highly esteemed. A good apricot, when perfectly ripe, is an excellent fruit. It has been somewhat condemned for its laxative qualities, but this has possibly arisen from the fruit having been eaten unripe, or in too great excess. Delicate persons should not eat the apricot uncooked, without a liberal allowance of powdered sugar. The apricot makes excellent jam and marmalade, and there are several foreign preparations of it which are considered great luxuries.

Flanc of Apricots, or Compôte of Apricots in a Raised Crust (Sweet Entremets)

Ingredients

¾ lb of short crust
From 9 to 12 good-sized apricots
¾ pint of water
½ lb of sugar

Mode

Make a short crust by one of the recipes on page 123 and line a mould with it. Boil the sugar and water together for 10 minutes;

halve the apricots, take out the stones and simmer them in the syrup until tender; watch them carefully and take them up the moment they are done, for fear they break. Arrange them neatly in the flanc or case; boil the syrup until reduced to a jelly, pour it over the fruit and serve either hot or cold. Greengages, plums of all kinds, peaches, etc., may be done in the same manner, as also currants, raspberries, gooseberries, strawberries, etc.; but with the last-named fruits, a little currant juice added to them will be found an improvement.

Time

Altogether, 1 hour to bake the flanc, about 10 minutes to simmer the apricots.
Sufficient for one entremets or side dish.

Baked Apricot Pudding

Ingredients

12 large apricots
¾ pint of breadcrumbs
1 pint of milk
3 oz of pounded sugar
The yolks of 4 eggs
1 glass of sherry

Mode

Make the milk boiling hot and pour it on to the breadcrumbs; when half cold, add the sugar, the well whisked yolks of the eggs and the sherry. Divide the apricots in half, scald them until they are soft and break them up with a spoon; then mix the fruit and other ingredients together, put a border of paste round the dish, fill with the mixture and bake the pudding from ½ to ¾ hour.

Time

½ to ¾ hour.
Sufficient for four or five persons.

Apricot Tart

Ingredients

12 or 14 apricots
Sugar to taste
Puff paste or short crust

Mode

Break the apricots in half, take out the stones and put them in to a pie dish, in the centre of which place a very small cup or jar, bottom uppermost; sweeten with good moist sugar, but add no water. Line the edge of the dish with paste, put on the cover and ornament the pie in any of the usual modes. Bake from ½ to ¾ hour, according to size; and if puff paste is used, glaze it about 10 minutes before the pie is done and put it into the oven again to set the glaze. Short crust merely requires a little sifted sugar sprinkled over it before being sent to table.

Time

½ to ¾ hour.
Sufficient for four or five persons.

Barberries

A fruit of such great acidity that even birds refuse to eat it. In this respect, it nearly approaches the tamarind. When boiled with sugar, it makes a very agreeable preserve or jelly, according to the different modes of preparing it. Barberries are also used as a dry sweetmeat, and in sugarplums or confits, are pickled with vinegar and are used for various culinary purposes. They are well calculated to allay heat and thirst in persons afflicted with fevers. The berries, arranged on

BARBERRIES.

bunches of nice curled parsley, make an exceedingly pretty garnish for supper dishes, particularly for white meats, like boiled fowl à la Béchamel, the three colours, scarlet, green and white, contrasting so well and producing a very good effect.

Barberry Tart

Ingredients

To every lb of barberries allow ¾ lb of lump sugar; paste.

Mode

Pick the barberries from the stalks and put the fruit into a stone jar; place this jar in boiling water and let it simmer very slowly until the fruit is soft, then put it into a preserving pan with the sugar and boil gently for 15 minutes; line a tartlet pan with paste, bake it, and, when the paste is cold, fill with the barberries, and, when the paste is cold, fill with the barberries, and ornament the tart with a few baked leaves of paste.

Time

¼ hour to bake the tart.

Carp

This species of fish inhabits the fresh waters, where they feed on worms, insects, aquatic plants, small fish, clay, or mould. Some of them are migratory. They have very small mouths and no teeth, and the gill membrane has three rays. The body is smooth and generally whitish. The carp both grows and increases very fast and is accounted the most valuable of all fish for the stocking of ponds. It has been pronounced the queen of river fish and was first introduced to this country about 300 years ago. Of its sound, or air bladder, a kind of glue is made, and a green paint of its gall.

THE CARP.

Baked Carp

Ingredients

1 carp
Forcemeat*
Breadcrumbs
1 oz butter
½ pint of stock
½ pint of port wine
6 anchovies
2 onions, sliced
1 bay leaf
A faggot of sweet herbs
Flour to thicken
The juice of 1 lemon
Cayenne and salt to taste
1 teaspoonful of powdered sugar

Mode

Stuff the carp with a delicate forcemeat, after thoroughly cleansing it and sew it up**, to prevent the stuffing from falling out. Rub it over with an egg, and sprinkle it with bread crumbs; lay it in a deep earthen dish, and drop the butter, oiled, over the breadcrumbs. Add the stock, onions, bay leaf, herbs, wine, and anchovies and bake for 1 hour. Put 1 oz of butter into a stewpan, melt it, and dredge in sufficient flour to dry it up; put in the strained liquor from the carp, stir frequently, and when it has boiled, add the lemon juice and seasoning. Serve the carp on a dish garnished with parsley and cut lemon, and the sauce in a boat.

Time

1¼ hours.
Sufficient for one or two persons.
*[Forcemeat for this dish would consist of butter, suet, bacon, herbs, onion, salt, nutmeg, cayenne, breadcrumbs and egg.]
**[Today we would probably not sew up the fish.]

Carrots

Carrots, says Liebig, contain the same kind of sugar as the juice of the sugarcane.

Baked or Boiled Carrot Pudding

Ingredients

½ lb of breadcrumbs
4 oz of suet
¼ lb of stoned raisins
¾ lb of carrots
¼ lb of currants
8 oz of sugar
3 eggs
Milk
¼ nutmeg

Mode

Boil the carrots until tender enough to mash to a pulp; add the remaining ingredients and moisten with sufficient milk to make the pudding of the consistency of thick batter. If to be boiled, put the mixture into a buttered basin, tie it down with a cloth and boil for 2½ hours; if to be baked, put it into a pie dish and bake for nearly an hour; turn it out of the dish, strew sifted sugar over it and serve.

Time

2½ hours to boil; 1 hour to bake.
Sufficient for five or six persons.

Cod

The Cod Tribe: The Jugular, characterised by bony gills, and ventral fins before the pectoral ones, commences the second of the Linnaean orders of fishes and is a numerous tribe, inhabiting only the depths of the ocean and seldom visiting the fresh waters. They have a smooth head and the gill membrane has seven rays. The body is oblong and covered with deciduous scales. The fins are all inclosed in skin, whilst their rays are unarmed. The ventral fins are slender, and terminate in a point. Their habits are gregarious and they feed on smaller fish and other marine animals.

The Season for Fishing Cod: The best season for catching cod is from the beginning of February to the end of April; and although each fisherman engaged in taking them, catches no

THE COD.

more than one at a time, an expert hand will sometimes take 400 in a day. The employment is excessively fatiguing, from the weight of the fish as well as from the coldness of the climate.

Cod Pie I (Economical)

Ingredients

Any remains of cold cod
12 oysters
Sufficient melted butter to moisten it
Mashed potatoes enough to fill up the dish

Mode

Flake the fish from the bone and carefully take away all the skin. Lay it in a pie dish, pour over the melted butter and oysters (or oyster sauce, if there is any left) and cover with mashed potatoes. Bake for ½ hour and send to table of a nice brown colour.

Time

½ hour.
Sufficient for four persons.

Cod Pie II

Ingredients

2 slices of cod
Pepper and salt to taste
½ a teaspoonful of grated nutmeg
1 large blade of pounded mace
2 oz of butter
½ pint of stock
A paste crust

For sauce:
1 tablespoonful of stock
¼ pint of cream or milk
Thickening of flour or butter

Lemon peel chopped very fine to taste
12 oysters

Mode

Lay the cod in salt for 4 hours, then wash it and place it in a dish; season and add the butter and stock; cover the crust and bake for 1 hour, or rather more. Now make the sauce, by mixing the ingredients named above; give it one boil, and pour it into the pie by a hole made at the top of the crust, which can easily be covered by a small piece of pastry cut and baked in any fanciful shape – such as a leaf, or otherwise.

Time

1½ hours.
Sufficient for six persons.

Note: The remains of cold fish may be used for this pie.

Damsons

Whether for jam, jelly, pie, pudding, water, ice, wine, dried fruit or preserved, the damson or *damascene* (for it was originally brought from Damascus, whence its name), is invaluable. It combines sugary and acid qualities in happy proportions, when full ripe. It is a fruit easily cultivated, and if budded 9 inches from the ground on vigorous stocks, it will grow several feet high in the first year and make fine standards the year following. Amongst the list of the best sorts of baking plums, the damson stands first, not only on account of the abundance of its juice but

DAMSONS.

also on account of its soon softening. Because of the roughness of its flavour, it requires a large quantity of sugar.

Baked Damsons for Winter Use

Ingredients

To every lb of fruit allow 6 oz of pounded sugar; melted mutton suet.

Mode

Choose sound fruit, not too ripe; pick off the stalks, weigh it, and to every lb allow the above proportion of pounded sugar. Put the fruit into large dry stone jars, sprinkling the sugar among it; cover the jars with saucers, place them in a rather cool oven and bake the fruit until it is quite tender. When cold, cover the top of the fruit with a piece of white paper [today we would use greaseproof paper] cut to the size of the jar; pour over this melted mutton suet about an inch thick, and cover the tops of the jars with thick brown paper, well tied down. Keep the jars in a cool dry place, and the fruit will remain good till the following Christmas but not much longer.

Time

From 5 to 6 hours to bake the damsons, in a very cool oven.

Damson Tart

Ingredients

1½ pints of damsons
¼ lb of moist sugar
½ lb of short or puff crust (see recipes on pages 107–109 and 123)

Mode

Put the damsons, with the sugar between them, into a deep pie dish, in the midst of which, place a small cup or jar turned upside down; pile the fruit high in the middle, line the edges of the dish with short or puff crust, whichever may be preferred; put on the cover, ornament the edges and bake from ½ to ¾ hour in a good oven. If puff crust is used, about 10 minutes before the pie is done, take it out of the oven, brush it over with the white of an egg beaten to a froth with the with the blade of a knife; strew some sifted sugar over, and a few drops of water, and put the tart back to finish baking: with shortcrust, a little plain sifted sugar, sprinkled over, is all that will be required.

Time

½ to ¾ hour.
Sufficient for five or six persons.

Game

Raised Pie of Poultry or Game

Ingredients

To every lb of flour allow ½ lb of butter, ½ pint of water, the yolks of 2 eggs, ½ teaspoonful of salt (these are for the crust)
1 large fowl or pheasant
A few slices of veal cutlet
A few slices of dressed ham
Forcemeat*
Seasoning of nutmeg
Allspice
Pepper and salt
Gravy

Mode

Make a stiff shortcrust with the above proportion of butter, flour, water and eggs and work it up very smoothly; butter a raised-pie mould, and line it with the paste. Previously to making the crust, bone the fowl, or whatever bird is intended to be used, lay it, breast downwards, upon a cloth, and season the inside well with pounded mace, allspice, pepper, and salt, then spread over it a layer of forcemeat, then a layer of seasoned veal, and then one of ham and then another layer of forcemeat and roll the fowl over, making the skin meet at the back. Line the pie with forcemeat, put in the fowl and fill up the cavities with slices of seasoned veal and ham and forcemeat; wet the edges of the pie, put on the cover, pinch the edges together with the paste pincers, and decorate it with leaves; brush it over with beaten yolk of egg and bake in a moderate oven for 4 hours. In the meantime, make a good strong gravy from the bones, pour it through a funnel into the hole at the top; cover this hole with a small leaf, and the pie, when cold, will be ready for use. Let it be remembered that the gravy must be considerably reduced before it is poured into the pie, as, when cold, it should form a firm jelly and not be the least degree in a liquid state. This recipe is suitable for all kinds of poultry or game, using one or more birds, according to the size of the pie intended to be made; but the birds must always be boned. Truffles, mushrooms, etc., added to this pie, make it much nicer, and, to enrich it, lard the fleshy parts of the poultry or game with thin strips of bacon. This method of forming raised pies in a mould is generally called a *timbale*, and has the advantage of being more easily made than one where the paste is raised by the hands; the crust, besides, being eatable.

Time

Large pie, 4 hours.
Seasonable: with poultry, all the year; with game, from September to March.
*[Forcemeat for a pie of this kind would consist of veal, bacon, salt, cayenne, mace, nutmeg, lemon peel, herbs and egg.]

Grouse

These birds are divided into wood grouse, black grouse, red grouse, and white grouse. The wood grouse is further distinguished as the cock of the wood, or capercalzie, and is as large as the turkey, being about 2 feet 9 inches in length, and weighing from 12 to 15 lbs. The female is considerably less than the male, and, in the colour of her feathers, differs widely from the other. This beautiful species is found principally in lofty, mountainous regions, and is very rare in Great Britain, but in the pine forests of Russia, Sweden, and other northern countries, it is very common. In these it has its habitat, feeding on the cones of the trees, and the fruits of various kinds of plants, especially the berry of the juniper. Black grouse is also distinguished as black game, or the black cock. It is not larger than the common hen, and weighs only about 4 lbs. The female is about ⅓ less than the male, and also differs considerably from hi in point of colour. Like the former, they are found chiefly in high situations, and are common in Russia, Siberia, and other northern countries. They are also found in the northern parts of Great Britain, feeding in winter on the various berries and fruits belonging to mountainous countries, and, in summer, frequently descending to the lower lands, to feed upon corn. The red grouse, gorcock, or moor cock, weighs about 19 oz, and the female somewhat less. In the wild heathy tracts of the northern counties of England it is plentiful, also in Wales and the Highlands of Scotland. Mr Pennant considered it peculiar to Britain, those found in the mountainous parts of Spain, France, and Italy, being only varieties of the same bird. White grouse, white game, or ptarmigan, is nearly the same size as the red grouse, and is found in lofty situations, where it supports itself in the severest weather. It is to be met with in most of the northern countries of Europe, and appears even in Greenland. In the Hebrides, Orkneys, and the Highlands of Scotland, it is also found, and sometimes, though rarely, among the fells of Northumberland and Cumberland. In winter they fly in flocks, and are so little familiar with the sight of man, that they are easily shot, and even snared. They feed on the wild produce of the hills, which sometimes imparts to their flesh a bitter, but not unpalatable, taste. According to Buffon, it is dark-coloured, and somewhat flavoured like the hare.

Grouse Pie

Ingredients

Grouse
Cayenne

Salt and pepper to taste
1 lb of rump steak
½ pint of well-seasoned broth
Puff paste

Mode

Line the bottom of a pie dish with the rump steak cut into neat pieces, and, should the grouse be large, cut them into joints, but, if small, they may be laid in the pie whole; season highly with salt, cayenne, and black pepper; pour in the broth and cover with a puff paste; brush the crust over with the yolk of an egg, and bake from ¾ to 1 hour. If the grouse is cut into joints, the backbones and trimmings will make the gravy, by stewing them with an onion, a little sherry, a bunch of herbs and a blade of mace, this should be poured in after the pie is baked.

Time

¾ to 1 hour.

Mushrooms

Varieties of the Mushroom: The common mushroom found in our pastures is the *Agaricus campestris* of science, and another

MUSHROOMS.

edible British species is *Agaricus Georgii*, but *Agaricus primulus* is affirmed to be the most delicious mushroom. The morel is *Morchella esculenta* and *Tuber cibarium* is the common truffle. There is New Zealand a long fungus, which grows from the head of a caterpillar, and which forms a horn, as it were, and is called *Sphaeria Robertsii*.

Baked Mushrooms (A Breakfast, Luncheon or Supper Dish)

Ingredients

16 to 20 mushroom flaps
Butter
Pepper to taste

Mode

For this mode of cooking, the mushroom flaps are better than the buttons and should not be too large. Cut off a portion of the stalk, peel the top and wipe the mushrooms carefully with a piece of flannel and a little fine salt. Put them into a tin baking dish, with a very small piece of butter placed on each mushroom; sprinkle over a little pepper and let them bake for about 20 minutes, or longer, should the mushrooms be very large. Have ready a very hot dish, pile the mushrooms high in the centre, pour the gravy round and send them to table quickly, with very hot plates.

Time

20 minutes; large mushrooms, ½ hour.
Sufficient for five or six persons.

Onions

The Genus Allium: The Onion, like the Leek, Garlic and Shalot, belongs to the genus *Allium* which is a numerous species of vegetable; and every one of them possesses, more or less, a volatile and acrid penetrating principle, pricking the thin transparent

ONION.

membrane of the eyelids, and all are very similar in their properties. In the whole of them, the bulb is the most active part, and any one of them may supply the place of the other, for they are all irritant, excitant and vesicant. With many, the onion is a very great favourite and is considered an extremely nutritive vegetable. The Spanish kind is frequently taken for supper, it being simply boiled, and then seasoned with salt, pepper and butter. Some dredge on a little flour, but many prefer it without this.

Baked Spanish Onions

Ingredients

4 or 5 Spanish onions
Salt
Water

Mode

Put the onions, with their skins on, into a saucepan of boiling water, slightly salted, and let them boil quickly for an hour. Then take them out, wipe them thoroughly, wrap each one in a piece of paper separately, and bake them in a moderate oven for 2 hours, or longer, should the onions be very large. They may be served in their skins and eaten with a piece of cold butter and a seasoning of pepper and salt; or they may be peeled and a good brown gravy poured over them.

Time

1 hour to boil; 2 hours to bake.
Sufficient for five or six persons.

Oysters

The Edible Oyster: This shellfish is almost universally distributed near the shores of seas in all latitudes, and they especially abound on the coasts of France and Britain. The coasts most celebrated, in England, for them, are those of Essex and Suffolk. Here they are

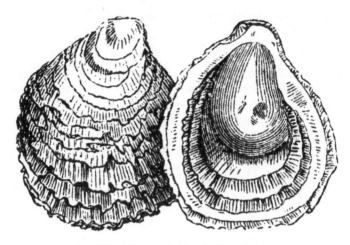

THE EDIBLE OYSTER.

dredged up by means of a net with an iron scraper at the mouth that is dragged by a rope from a boat over the beds. As soon as taken from their native beds, they are stored in pits, formed for the purpose, furnished with sluices, through which, at the spring tides, the water is suffered to flow. This water, being stagnant, soon becomes green in warm weather, and in a few days afterwards, the oysters acquire the same tinge, which increases their value in the market. They do not, however, attain their perfection and become fit for sale till the end of six or eight weeks. Oysters are not considered proper for the table till they are about a year and a half old; so that the brood of one spring are not to be taken for sale, till, at least, the September twelvemonth afterwards.

Fish and Oyster Pie

Ingredients

Any remains of cold fish, such as cod or haddock
2 dozen oysters
Pepper and salt to taste
Breadcrumbs sufficient for the quantity of fish
½ teaspoonful of grated nutmeg

1 teaspoonful of finely chopped parsley

Mode

Clear the fish from the bones and put a layer of it in a pie dish, which sprinkle with pepper and salt, then a layer of breadcrumbs, oysters, nutmeg and chopped parsley. Repeat this till the dish is quite full. You may form a covering either of breadcrumbs, which should be browned, or puff paste, which should be cut into long strips, and laid in crossbars over the fish, with a line of the paste first laid round the edge. Before putting on the top, pour in some melted butter, or a little thin white sauce, and the oyster liquor, and bake.

Time

If made of cooked fish, ¼ hour; if made of fresh fish and puff paste, ¾ hour.

Note: A nice little dish may be made by flaking any cold fish, adding a few oysters, seasoning with pepper and salt and covering with mashed potatoes; ¼ hour will bake it.

Pears

The pear, like the apple, is indigenous to this country, but the wild pear is a very unsatisfactory fruit. The best varieties were brought from the East by the Romans, who cultivated them with care and probably introduced some of their best sorts into this island, to which others were added by the inhabitants of the monasteries. The Dutch and Flemings, as well as the French, have excelled in the cultivation of the pear, and most of the late varieties introduced are from France and Flanders. The pear is a hardy tree and a longer liver than the apple: it has been known to exist for centuries. There are now about 150 varieties of this fruit. Though perfectly wholesome when ripe, the pear is not so when green, but in this state, it is fit for stewing. An agreeable beverage, called perry, is made from pears, and the varieties which are least fit for eating make the best perry.

The *Bon Chrétien* Pear: The valuable variety of pear called *Bon Chrétien*, which comes to our tables in winter, either raw or cooked, received its name through the following incident: Louis XI, king of France, had sent for Saint François de Paule from the lower part of Calabria, in the hopes of recovering his health through his intercession. The saint brought with him the seeds of this pear, and, as he was called at court *Le Bon Chrétien*, this fruit obtained the name of him to whom France owed its introduction.

Baked Pears

Ingredients

12 pears
The rind of 1 lemon
6 cloves
10 whole allspice
To every pint of water allow ½ lb of loaf sugar

Mode

Pare and cut the pears into halves and, should they be very large, into quarters; leave the stalks on and carefully remove the cores. Place them in a clean baking jar, with a closely fitting lid; add to them the lemon rind cut in strips, the juice of ½ lemon, the cloves, pounded allspice and sufficient water just to cover the whole, with sugar in the above proportion. Cover the jar down closely, put it into a very cool oven and bake the pears from 5 to 6 hours, but be very careful that the oven is not too hot. To improve the colour of the fruit, a few drops of prepared cochineal may be added; but this will not be found necessary if the pears are very gently baked.

Time

Large pears, 5 to 6 hours, in a very slow oven.
Sufficient for seven or eight persons.

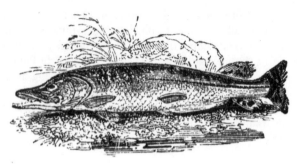

THE PIKE.

Pike

This fish is, on account of its voracity, termed the freshwater shark and is abundant in most of the European lakes, especially those of the northern parts. It grows to an immense size, some attaining to the measure of 8 feet, in Lapland and Russia. The smaller lakes of this country and Ireland, vary in the kinds of fish they produce; some affording trout, others pike and so on. Where these happen to be together, however, the trout soon becomes extinct. 'Within a short distance of Castlebar,' says a writer on sports, 'there is a small bog lake called Derreens. Ten years ago, it was celebrated for its numerous well-sized trouts. Accidentally pike effected a passage into the lake from the Minola river, and now the trouts are extinct, or, at least, none of them are caught or seen. Previous to the intrusion, collective weight often amounted to twenty pounds.' As an eating fish, the pike is in general dry.

Baked Pike

Ingredients

1 or 2 pike
A nice delicate stuffing
1 egg
Breadcrumbs
¼ lb butter

Mode

Scale the fish, take out the gills, wash and wipe it thoroughly dry; stuff it with forcemeat, sew it up* and fasten the tail in the mouth by means of a skewer; brush it over with egg, sprinkle with breadcrumbs and baste with butter, before putting it in the oven, which must be well heated. When the pike is of a nice brown colour, cover it with buttered paper, as the outside would become dry. If two are dressed, a little variety may be made by making one of them green with a little chopped parsley mixed with the breadcrumbs. Serve anchovy or Dutch sauce and plain melted butter with it.

Time

According to size, 1 hour, more or less.
*[Today we would probably not sew up the fish.]

Plums

Almost all the varieties of the cultivated plum are agreeable and refreshing; it is not a nourishing fruit and, if indulged in to excess

PLUMS.

when unripe, is almost certain to cause diarrhoea and cholera. Weak and delicate persons had better abstain from plums altogether. The modes of preparing plums are as numerous as the varieties of the fruit. The objections raised against raw plums do not apply to the cooked fruit, which even the invalid may eat in moderation.

The wild sloe is the parent of the plum, but the acclimated kinds come from the East. The cultivation of this fruit was probably attended to very early in England, as Gerrard informs us that, in 1597, he had in his garden, in Holborn, threescore sorts. The sloe is a shrub common in our hedgerows and belongs to the natural order *Amygdaleae*; the fruit is about the size of a large pea, of a black colour and covered with a bloom of a bright blue. It is one of the few indigenous to our island. The juice is extremely sharp and astringent, and was formerly employed as a medicine, where astringents were necessary. It now assists in the manufacture of a red wine made to imitate port and also for adulteration. The leaves have been used to adulterate tea, and the fruit, when ripe, makes a good preserve.

Plum Tart

Ingredients

½ lb of good short crust
1½ pints of plums
¼ lb of moist sugar

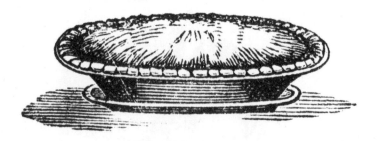

PLUM TART.

Mode

Line the edges of a deep tart dish with crust made by the recipe on page 123; fill the dish with plums and place a small cup or jar, upside down, in the midst of them. Put in the sugar, cover the pie with crust, ornament the edges and bake in a good oven from ½ to ¾ hour. When puff crust is preferred to short crust, use that made by the recipe above, and glaze the top by brushing it over with the white of an egg beaten to a stiff froth with a knife; sprinkle over a little sifted sugar and put the pie in the oven to set the glaze.

Time

½ to ¾ hour.
Sufficient for five or six persons.

Sweet Vol-au-Vent of Plums, Apples or Any Other Fresh Fruit

Ingredients

I lb of puff paste
About 1 pint of fruit compote

Mode

Make ½ lb of puff paste by the recipe on page 107, taking care to bake it in a good brisk oven, to draw it up nicely and make it look light. Have ready sufficient stewed fruit, the syrup of which must be boiled down until very thick; fill the vol-au-vent with this and pile it high in the centre; powder a little sugar over it and put it back in the oven to glaze, or use a salamander for the purpose: the vol-au-vent is then ready to serve. They may be made with any fruit that is in season, such as rhubarb, oranges, gooseberries, currants, cherries, apples, etc., but care must be taken not to have the syrup too thin, for fear of its breaking through the crust.

Time

½ hour to 40 minutes to bake the vol-au-vent.
Sufficient for 1 entremets.

Rabbit

The Common or Wild Rabbit: Warrens, or inclosures, are frequently made in favourable localities, and some of them are so large as to comprise 2,000 acres. The common wild rabbit is of a grey colour and is esteemed the best for the purposes of food. Its skin is valuable as an article of commerce, being used for the making of hats. Another variety of the rabbit, however, called the 'silver grey', has been lately introduced to this country and is still more valuable. Its colour is a black ground, thickly interspersed with grey hairs, and its powers as a destroyer and consumer of vegetable food are well known to be enormous, especially by those who have gardens in the vicinity a rabbit warren.

Rabbit Pie

Ingredients

1 rabbit
A few slices of ham
Salt and white pepper to taste
2 blades of pounded mace
½ teaspoonful of grated nutmeg
A few forcemeat* balls
3 hard-boiled eggs
½ pint of gravy
Puff crust

Mode

Cut up the rabbit (which should be young), remove the breastbone, and bone the legs. Put the rabbit, slices of ham, forcemeat balls, and hard eggs, by turns, in layers, and season each layer with pepper, salt, pounded mace, and grated nutmeg. Pour in about ½ pint of water, cover with crust and bake in a well-heated oven for about 1½ hours. Should the crust acquire too much colour, place a piece of paper over it to prevent its burning. When done, pour in at the top, by means of the hole in the middle of the crust, a little good gravy, which may be made of the breast and leg bones of the rabbit and two or three shank bones, flavoured with onion, herbs and spices.

Time

1½ hours.
Sufficient for five or six persons.
*[Forcemeat for a pie of this type would consists of bacon, suet, lemon rind, herbs, salt, cayenne, mace, breadcrumbs and egg.]

Meat or Sausage Rolls

Ingredients

1 lb of puff paste
Sausagemeat
The yolk of 1 egg

Mode

Make 1 lb of puff paste by the recipe on page 108; roll it out to the thickness of about ½ inch, or rather less, and divide it into eight, ten, or twelve squares, according to the size the rolls are intended to be. Place some sausage meat on one half of each square, wet the edges of the paste and fold it over the meat; slightly press the edges together, and trim them neatly with a knife. Brush the rolls over with the yolk of an egg, and bake them in a well-heated oven for about ½ an hour, or longer should they be very large.

Time

½ an hour, or longer if the rolls are large.
Sufficient: 1 lb of paste for ten or twelve rolls.
Seasonable: with sausage meat, from September to March or April.

Winter

Christmas

Christmas Cake

Ingredients

5 teacupfuls of flour
1 teacupful of melted butter
1 teacupful of cream
1 teacupful of treacle
1 teacupful of moist sugar
2 eggs
½ oz of powdered ginger
½ lb of raisins
1 teaspoonful of carbonate of soda
1 tablespoonful of vinegar

Mode

Make the butter sufficiently warm to melt it but do not allow it to oil; put the flour into a basin; add to it the sugar, ginger and raisins, which should be stoned and cut into small pieces. When these dry ingredients are thoroughly mixed, stir in the butter, cream, treacle and well-whisked eggs and beat the mixture for a few minutes. Dissolve the soda in the vinegar, add it to the dough, and be particular that these latter ingredients are well incorporated with the others; put the cake into a buttered mould or tin, place it in a moderate oven immediately and bake it for 1¾ to 2¼ hours.

Time

1¾ to 2¼ hours.

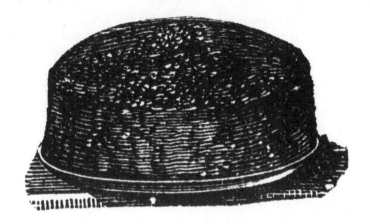

HOLIDAY CAKE.

Good Holiday Cake

Ingredients

1½ *d* worth of Borwick's German baking powder
2 lbs of flour
6 oz of butter
¼ lb of lard
1 lb of currants
½ lb of stoned and cut raisins
¼ lb of mixed candied peel
½ lb of moist sugar
3 eggs
¾ pint of cold milk

Mode

Mix the baking powder with the flour, then rub in the butter and lard; have ready the currants, washed, picked and dried, the raisins stoned and cut into small pieces (not chopped) and the peel cut into neat slices. Add these with the sugar to the flour, etc., and mix all the dry ingredients well together. Whisk the eggs, stir to them the milk and with this liquid moisten the cake; beat it up well, that all may be very thoroughly mixed; line a cake tin with buttered paper, put in the cake and bake it from 2½ to 2¾ hours in a good oven. To ascertain when it is done, plunge a clean knife into the middle of it, and if, on withdrawing it, the knife looks clean, and not sticky, the cake is done. To prevent its burning at the top, a piece of clean paper may be put over whilst the cake is soaking or being thoroughly cooked in the middle. A steamer, such as is used for steaming potatoes, makes a very good cake tin, if it be lined at the bottom and sides with buttered paper.

Time

2¼ to 2¾ hours.

Mincemeat

Ingredients

2 lbs of raisins
3 lbs of currants
1½ lbs of lean beef
3 lbs of beef suet
2 lbs of moist sugar
2 oz of citron
2 oz of candied lemon peel
2 oz of candied orange peel
1 small nutmeg
1 pottle of apples*
The rind of 2 lemons
The juice of 1 lemon
½ pint of brandy

Mode

Stone and cut the raisins once or twice across, but do not chop them; wash, dry and pick the currants free from stalks and grit and mince the beef and suet, taking care that the latter is chopped very fine; slice the citron and candied peel, grate the nutmeg and pare, core and mince the apples; mince the lemon peel, strain the juice and when all the ingredients are thus prepared, mix them well together, adding the brandy when the other things are well blended; press the whole into a jar, carefully exclude the air, and the mincemeat will be ready for use in a fortnight.

Note: Make this about the beginning of December.
*[A pottle is generally defined as half a gallon, or 4 pints.]

Excellent Mincemeat

Ingredients

3 large lemons
3 large apples
1 lb of currants
1 lb of suet
2 lbs of moist sugar
1 oz of sliced candied citron
1 oz of sliced candied orange peel, and the same quantity of lemon peel
1 teacupful of brandy
2 tablespoonfuls of orange marmalade

Mode

Grate the rinds of the lemons; squeeze out the juice, strain it and boil the remainder of the lemons until tender enough to pulp or chop very finely. Then add to this pulp the apples, which should be baked, and their skins and cores removed; put in the remaining ingredients one by one, and, as they are added, mix everything very thoroughly together. Put the mincemeat into a stone jar with a closely fitting lid, and in a fortnight will be ready for use.

Note: This should be made the first or second week in December.

MINCE PIES.

Mince Pies

Ingredients

Good puff paste
Mincemeat

Mode

Make some good puff paste by the recipe on page 109; roll it out to the thickness of about ¼ inch, and line some good-sized pattypans with it; fill them with mincemeat, cover with the paste, and cut it off all round close to the edge of the tin. Put the pies into a brisk oven, to draw the paste up, and bake for 25 minutes, or longer, should the pies be very large; brush them over with the white of an egg, beaten with the blade of a knife to a stiff froth; sprinkle over pounded sugar, and put them into the oven for a minute or two, to dry the egg; dish the pies on a white d'oyley, and serve hot. They may be merely sprinkled with pounded sugar instead of being glazed, when that mode is preferred. To rewarm them, put the pies on the pattypans, and let them remain in the oven for 10 minutes or ¼ hour, and they will be almost good as if freshly baked.

Time

25 to 30 minutes; 10 minutes to rewarm.

Sufficient

½ lb of paste for 4 pies.

Ginger/Ground Ginger

Rich Sweetmeat Gingerbread Nuts

Ingredients

1 lb of treacle
¼ lb of clarified butter
1 lb of coarse brown sugar
2 oz of ground ginger
1 oz of candied orange peel
1 oz of candied angelica
½ oz of candied lemon peel
½ oz of coriander seeds
½ oz of caraway seeds
1 egg
Flour

Mode

Put the treacle into a basin, pour over it the butter, melted so as not to oil, the sugar and ginger. Stir these ingredients well together and, whilst mixing, add the candied peel, which should be cut into very small pieces, but not bruised, and the caraway and coriander seeds, which should be pounded. Having mixed all thoroughly together, break in an egg, and work the whole up with as much fine flour as may be necessary to form a paste. Make this into nuts of any size, put them on a tin plate, and bake in a slow oven from ¼ to ½ hour.

Time

¼ to ½ hour.

Thick Gingerbread

Ingredients

1 lb of treacle
¼ of butter
¼ of coarse brown sugar
1½ lbs of flour
1 oz of ginger
½ oz of ground allspice
1 teaspoonful of carbonate of soda
¼ pint of warm milk
3 eggs

Mode

Put the flour into a basin, with the sugar, ginger and allspice; mix these together; warm the butter and add it, with the treacle, to the other ingredients. Stir well; make the milk just warm, dissolve the carbonate of soda in it and mix the whole into a nice smooth dough with the eggs, which should be previously well whisked; pour the mixture into a buttered tin and bake it from ¾ to 1 hour, or longer, should the gingerbread be very thick. Just before it is done, brush the top over with the yolk of an egg beaten up with a little milk, and put it back in the oven to finish baking.

Time

¾ to 1 hour.

Sunderland Gingerbread Nuts

Ingredients

1¾ lbs treacle
1 lb of moist sugar
1 lb of butter
2¾ lbs of flour
1½ oz of ground ginger

1½ oz of allspice
1½ oz of coriander seeds

Mode

Let the allspice, coriander seeds and ginger be freshly ground; put them into a basin with the flour and sugar and mix these ingredients well together; warm the treacle and butter together; then with a spoon work it into the flour, etc., until the whole forms a nice smooth paste. Drop the mixture from the spoon on to a piece of buttered paper and bake in rather a slow oven from 20 minutes to ½ hour. A little candied lemon peel mixed with the above is an improvement, and a great authority in culinary matters suggests the addition of a little cayenne pepper in gingerbread. Whether it be advisable to use this latter ingredient or not, we leave our readers to decide.

Time

20 minutes to ½ hour.

White Gingerbread

Ingredients

1 lb of flour
½ lb of butter
½ lb of loaf sugar
The rind of 1 lemon
1 oz of ground ginger
1 nutmeg, grated
½ teaspoonful of carbonate of soda
1 gill* of milk

Mode

Rub the butter into the flour; add the sugar, which should be finely pounded and sifted, and the minced lemon rind, ginger and nutmeg. Mix these well together; make the milk just warm, stir in the soda and work the whole into a nice smooth paste; roll it out, cut it into cakes and bake in a moderate oven from 15 to 20 minutes.

Time

15 to 20 minutes.
*[A gill is generally defined as ¼ pint.]

Lark

Lark Pie (an Entrée)

Ingredients

A few thin slices of beef
The same of bacon
9 larks
Flour

For stuffing:
1 teacupful of breadcrumbs
½ teaspoonful of minced lemon peel
1 teaspoonful of minced parsley
1 egg
Salt and pepper to taste
1 teaspoonful of chopped shalot
½ pint of weak stock or water
Puff paste

Mode

Make a stuffing of breadcrumbs, minced lemon peel, parsley and the yolk of an egg, all of which should be well mixed together; roll the larks in flour and stuff them. Line the bottom of a pie dish with a few slices of beef and bacon; over these place the larks and season with salt, pepper, minced parsley, and chopped shalot, in the above proportion. Pour in the stock or water, cover with crust and bake for 1 hour in a moderate oven. During the time the pie is baking, shake it two or three times, to assist in thickening the gravy, and serve very hot.

Time

1 hour.
Sufficient for five or six persons.

Orange

Citrus Aurantium: The principal varieties are the sweet, or China orange, and the bitter, or Seville orange; the Maltese is also worthy of notice, from its red blood-like pulp. The orange is extensively cultivated in the south of Europe, and in Devonshire, on walls with a south aspect, it bears an abundance of fruit. So great is the increase in the demand for the orange, and so ample the supply, that it promises to rival the apple in its popularity. The orange tree is considered young at the age of a hundred years. The pulp of the orange consists of a collection of oblong vesicles filled with a sugary and refreshing juice. The orange blossom is proverbially chosen for the bridal wreath, and, from the same flower, an essential oil is extracted, hardly less esteemed than the celebrated ottar of roses. Of all marmalades, that made from the Seville orange is the best. The peel and juice of the orange are much used in culinary preparations. From oranges are made preserves, comfitures, jellies, glacés, sherbet, liqueurs and syrups. The juice of the orange in a glass *d'eau sucrée* makes a refreshing and wholesome drink. From the clarified pulp of the orange, the French make a delicious jelly, which they serve in small pots and call *crème*. The rasped peel of the orange is used in several sweet *entremets*, to which it communicates its perfume. The confectioner manufactures a variety of dainties from all parts of the orange. Confections of orange peel are excellent tonics and stomachics. Persons with delicate stomachs should abstain from oranges at dessert, because their acidity is likely to derange the digestive organs.

The Orange in Portugal: The Orange known under the name of 'Portugal Orange' comes originally from China. Not more than two centuries ago, the Portuguese brought thence the first scion, which has multiplied so prodigiously that we now see entire forests of orange trees in Portugal.

Oranges and Cloves: It appears to have been the custom formerly, in England, to make new year's presents with oranges stuck full with cloves. We read in one of Ben Jonson's pieces, the 'Christmas Masque', 'He has an orange and rosemary, but not a clove to stick in it'.

Baked Orange Pudding

Ingredients

6 oz of stale sponge cake or bruised ratafias
6 oranges
1 pint of milk
6 eggs
½ lb of sugar

Mode

Bruise the sponge cake or ratafias into fine crumbs and pour upon them the milk, which should be boiling. Rub the rinds of two of the oranges on sugar, and add this, with the juice of the remainder, to the other ingredients. Beat up the eggs, stir them in, sweeten to taste and put the mixture into a pie dish previously lined with puff paste. Bake for rather more than ½ hour; turn it out of the dish, strew sifted sugar over and serve.

Time

Rather more than ½ hour.
Sufficient for three or four persons.

Orange Batter Pudding

Ingredients

4 eggs
1 pint of milk
1½ oz of loaf sugar
3 tablespoonfuls of flour

Mode

Make the batter with the above ingredients, put it into a well-buttered basin, tie it down with a cloth and boil for 1 hour. As soon as it is turned out of the basin, put a small jar of orange marmalade all over the top and send the pudding very quickly to table.

Time

1 hour.
Sufficient for five or six persons.

Raisin Grape

All the kinds of raisins have much the same virtues; they are nutritive and balsamic, but they are very subject to fermentation with juices of any

RAISIN-GRAPE.

kind; and hence, when eaten immoderately, they often bring on colics. There are many varieties of grape used for raisins; the fruit of Valencia is that mostly dried for culinary purposes, whilst most of the table kinds are grown in Malaga and called Muscatels. The finest of all table raisins come from Provence or Italy; the most esteemed of all are those of Roquevaire; they are very large and very sweet. This sort is rarely eaten by any but the most wealthy. The dried Malaga, or Muscatel raisins, which come to this country packed in small boxes, and nicely preserved in bunches, are variable in their quality, but mostly of a rich flavour, when new, juicy, and of a deep purple hue.

Baked Plum Pudding

Ingredients

2 lbs of flour
1 lb of currants
1 lb of raisins
1 lb of suet
2 eggs
1 pint of milk
A few slices of candied peel

Mode

Chop the suet finely; mix with it the flour, currants, stoned raisins and candied peel; moisten with the well-beaten eggs and add sufficient milk to make the pudding of the consistency of very thick batter. Put it into a buttered dish and bake in a good oven from 2¼ to 2½ hours; turn it out, strew sifted sugar over and serve. For a very plain pudding, use only half the quantity of fruit, omit the eggs and substitute milk or water for them. The above ingredients make a large family pudding; for a small one, half the quantity would be found ample, but it must be baked quite 1½ hours.

Time

Large pudding, 2¼ to 2½ hours; half the size, 1½ hours.
Sufficient for nine or ten persons.

Soyer's Sauce for Plum Pudding

Ingredients

The yolks of 3 eggs
1 tablespoonful of powdered sugar
1 gill* of milk
A very little grated lemon rind
2 small wineglassfuls of brandy

Mode

Separate the yolks from the whites of 3 eggs and put the former into a stewpan; add the sugar, milk and grated lemon rind, and stir over the fire until the mixture thickens; but do not allow it to boil. Put in the brandy; let the sauce stand by the side of the fire, to get quite hot; keep stirring it, and serve in a boat or tureen separately or pour it over the pudding.

Time

Altogether, 10 minutes.
Sufficient for six or seven persons.
*[A gill is generally defined as ¼ pint.]

Pork Pies (Warwickshire Recipe)

Ingredients

For the crust:
5 lbs of lard to 14 lbs of flour
Milk
Water

For filling the pies:
To every 3 lbs of meat allow 1 oz of salt
2¼ oz of pepper
A small quantity of cayenne
1 pint of water

Mode

Rub into the flour a portion of the lard; the remainder put with sufficient milk and water to mix the crust and boil this gently for ¼ hour. Pour it boiling on the flour, and knead and beat it till perfectly smooth. Now raise the crust in either a round or oval form, cut up the pork into pieces the size of a nut, season it in the above proportion and press it compactly into the pie, in alternate layers of fat and lean and pour in a small quantity of water; lay on the lid, cut the edges smoothly round and pinch them together. Bake in a brick oven, which should be slow, as the meat is very solid. Very frequently, the inexperienced cook finds much difficulty in raising the crust. She should bear in mind that it must not be allowed to get cold or it will fall immediately: to prevent this, the operation should be performed as near the fire as possible. As considerable dexterity and expertness are necessary to raise the crust with the hand only, a glass bottle or small jar may be placed in the middle of the paste, and the crust moulded on this; but be particular that it is kept warm the whole time.

Sufficient

The proportions for one pie are 1 lb of flour and 3 lbs of meat.

Baked Rice Pudding I

Ingredients

1 small teacupful of rice
4 eggs
1 pint of milk
2 oz of fresh butter
2 oz of beef marrow
¼ lb of currants
2 tablespoonfuls of brandy
Nutmeg
¼ lb of sugar
The rind of ½ lemon

Mode

Put the lemon rind and milk into a stewpan and let it infuse till the milk is well flavoured with the lemon; in the meantime, boil the rice until tender in water, with a very small quantity of salt and, when done, let it be thoroughly drained. Beat the eggs, stir to them the milk, which should be strained, the butter, marrow, currants and remaining ingredients; add the rice, and mix all well together. Line the edges of the dish with puff paste, put in the pudding, and bake for about ¾ hour in a slow oven. Slices of candied peel may be added at pleasure, or sultana raisins may be substituted for the currants.

Time

¾ hour.
Sufficient for five or six persons.

Seasonable: Suitable for a winter pudding, when fresh fruits are not obtainable.

Baked Rice Pudding II (Plain and Economical; a Nice Pudding for Children)

Ingredients

1 teacupful of rice
2 tablespoonfuls of moist sugar
1 quart of milk
½ oz of butter or 2 small tablespoonfuls of chopped suet
½ teaspoonful of grated nutmeg

Mode

Wash the rice, put it into a pie dish with the sugar, pour in the milk and stir these ingredients well together; then add the butter, cut up into very small pieces or, instead of this, the above proportion of finely minced suet; grate a little nutmeg over the top and bake the pudding in a moderate oven from 1½ to 2 hours. As the rice is not previously cooked, care must be taken that the pudding be very slowly baked, to give plenty of time for the rice to swell, and for it to be very thoroughly done.

Time

1½ to 2 hours.
Sufficient for five or six persons.

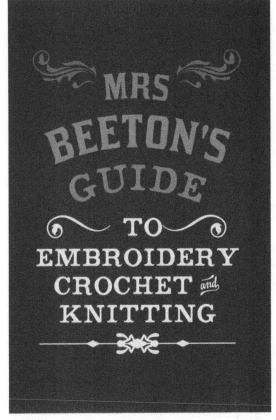

Mrs Beeton's Guide to Embroidery, Crochet and
Knitting

Isabella Beeton

Containing over 200 unique patterns alongside clear and engaging
descriptions of key techniques, this is an essential volume for anyone
with an interest in vintage fashion and needlework.

978 1 4456 4422 6

192 pages, illustrated throughout